The Unlikely Sto...
Museum of Appalachia
and How It Came To Be

For my daughter, Elaine Irwin Meyer;
and my three grandchildren,
Lindsey Meyer Gallaher,
John Rice Irwin Meyer,
and Will Meyer

Dedicated to my late wife, Elizabeth,
and to my late daughter, Karen Irwin Erickson

Other Schiffer Books By The Author:
Alex Stewart: Portrait of a Pioneer. ISBN: 0887400531. $14.99
Baskets and Basketmakers in Southern Appalachia. ISBN: 0916838617. $19.95
Guns and Gunmaking Tools of Southern Appalachia. ISBN: 0916838811. $14.95
Musical Instruments of the Southern Appalachian Mountains. ISBN: 0916838803. $14.99
A People and Their Music. ISBN: 0764309420. $29.95
A People and Their Quilts. ISBN: 0916838870. $45.00

Other Schiffer Books on Related Subjects:
Making Colorful Corn Shuck Dolls. Anne Freels. ISBN: 978-0-7643-3935-6. $16.99

Cover Design: Bruce Waters
Type set in Americana XBd BT/Arrus BT

ISBN: 978-0-7643-4114-4
Printed in China

Schiffer Books are available at special discounts for bulk purchases for sales promotions or premiums. Special editions, including personalized covers, corporate imprints, and excerpts can be created in large quantities for special needs. For more information contact the publisher:

Published by Schiffer Publishing Ltd.
4880 Lower Valley Road
Atglen, PA 19310
Phone: (610) 593-1777; Fax: (610) 593-2002
E-mail: Info@schifferbooks.com

For the largest selection of fine reference books on this and related subjects, please visit our website at **www. schifferbooks.com**
We are always looking for people to write books on new and related subjects. If you have an idea for a book, please contact us at
proposals@schifferbooks.com

This book may be purchased from the publisher.
Include $5.00 for shipping.
Please try your bookstore first.
You may write for a free catalog.

In Europe, Schiffer books are distributed by
Bushwood Books
6 Marksbury Ave.
Kew Gardens
Surrey TW9 4JF England
Phone: 44 (0) 20 8392 8585; Fax: 44 (0) 20 8392 9876
E-mail: info@bushwoodbooks.co.uk
Website: www.bushwoodbooks.co.uk

Front Cover Photo: Museum Founder John Rice Irwin with his mandolin and his dog. (photo by Robin Hood, Pulitzer Prize winner)

EARLY MORNING AT THE MUSEUM OF APPALACHIA (Museum staff photo)

Contents

Acknowledgments

My dear friend Alex Haley was fond of quoting an old proverb: "When you see a turtle setting on top of a fence post, you know he's had a lot of help." That old saying is particularly applicable to me with regard to the building of the Museum of Appalachia. I'm listing here (in alphabetical order) a few of the kind souls who come to mind in their unselfish contributions to the health and welfare of the Museum of Appalachia:

David Campbell is my most capable aide, a retired educator who has learned to decipher my handwritten scribbling (in some cases better than I'm able to do) and who transposed it into a somewhat legible form.

My immediate family, including my late wife, Elizabeth M. Irwin, and my two daughters, Elaine and the late Karen, who were champions of support through all the years of the growth and development of the Museum. Elizabeth is perhaps most deserving for any success I've had in all my many endeavors because of her steadfast acquiescence as I moved through the maze of uncertainty that accompanies any new territory. Elaine, our youngest daughter, was remarkably supportive in the early years and later Elaine took up the "torch," so to speak, and became the able executive director and then president of the Museum. Her dedication to me and to the Museum has been a godsend, and I'm extremely grateful to her for carrying on the tradition.

My grandchildren: Lindsey Gallaher, John Rice Irwin Meyer, and Will Meyer. When all is said and done, there is no greater gift a person can hold dearer than having admiring and loving grandchildren, and I'm grateful to Elaine and her husband Ed Meyer for these three beautiful and loving offspring.

Andrea Fritts was my able assistant for 34 years and wore multiple hats as my secretary, administrative assistant, supporter, and friend.

Robin Hood, the Pulitzer Prize-winning photographer whose stellar photographic images became silent recorders of our many travels into the hinterlands of Southern Appalachia for years, and who took countless photos of "our people." I first met Robin in Governor Alexander's office in Nashville, and we soon became best friends. Several of my published books contain Robin's photos, and he and his family remain fast friends. I'm much indebted to him for his contribution to the Museum and for capturing the images of so many of my old mountain friends. He and I have collaborated on numerous books and articles.

Billy Kennedy is a noted historian and journalist from Northern Ireland and a steadfast supporter of the Museum of Appalachia. He is the author of ten books on great Americans, especially those of the Southern Appalachians, whose roots go back to Northern Ireland. He has allowed me to write the foreword of each book.

Mickey Lindsey, who has, for some twenty-five years, been in charge of the outdoor gardens and grounds of the Museum, and who has provided the "muscle" in moving many items to the Museum.

Lou Nolan, who labored diligently with editing and layout of the book in its early stages.

Carol Ostrom, my long-time associate, first in her class at the University of Tennessee, who provided superb and persistent assistance not only in matters of punctuation, grammar, and technical details, but also in suggesting substantive judgmental and organizational changes.

Jim Marziotti, a true master in restoring old and faded photographs, and in positioning them in the text. He is a genius in utilizing all the modern technology.

Jill Peterson of Texas is the founder and publisher of the nationally popular magazine, *Simple Living*, and has encouraged me "unmercifully" regarding this book.

Dean Stone is the editor of the *Maryville Times* newspaper. He was the first photographer/feature writer to do pictures and stories of the Museum of Appalachia, beginning in 1965. He remains a great supporter; he has written numerous features and positive editorials on the Museum.

Bill Henry, the noted whittler, has helped me ferret out hundreds of interesting and historical items from the region for the Museum.

David Irwin, my brother, has been a lifelong "assistant" and is referred to numerous times in the text of the book.

Gene Purcell is referred to in the book as "my closest friend and greatest benefactor." He is responsible for putting me on the trail of thousands of mountain artifacts and mountain people.

David Byrd, from the mountains of upper East Tennessee, has assisted me in purchasing literally thousands of Appalachian relics; and he has assisted me and the Museum in untold ways.

Jack Williams has attended and assisted with many meetings and gatherings involving the Museum; and he has documented these events in thousands of stellar photographs.

Richard Doub has meticulously restored, in a remarkably professional and accomplished manner, numerous old and faded photographs. He has also captured, on an ongoing basis, a plethora of images of the Museum and its activities.

Frank Hoffman, a professional photographer and longtime friend, has traveled many thousands of miles with me, visiting and photographing the rural mountain folk of Southern Appalachia; he has restored many seemingly "un-restorable" damaged and mutilated photographs to near perfect condition.

David West, of radio and television fame, is a close friend and accomplished banjo player who has performed with my band for many years. He promotes the Museum "ever chance he gets."

Members of John Rice Irwin's Museum of Appalachia Band, who, for some thirty-five years, have entertained groups visiting the Museum.

Shirley DeMarcus, a cherished neighbor and helpmate. Any time the Museum becomes overrun with an influx of visitors, or needs help with events, she responds promptly to our call for help.

Carl "Ramrod" Bell is strictly a "mountain boy" who knows and assists with every outdoor aspect of the Museum—gardening, animal care, farming, repairs and maintenance, and other practical and necessary chores.

The Museum of Appalachia staff, the most friendly, efficient, and capable people with whom I've worked.

"My good friend, and distant cousin, John Rice Irwin is responsible for one of my favorite Tennessee treasures—The Museum of Appalachia in Norris.

John Rice has dedicated his life to collecting, preserving, and exhibiting the artifacts of our strongly independent and ever resourceful forefathers who settled this unique region of our country.

I think you will enjoy traveling through time by reading the congruent stories of John Rice and the Museum of Appalachia, and how he managed to acquire one of the largest collections of heirlooms that depict pioneer life in early Appalachia.

I hope you enjoy it as much as I have."

Senator Howard H. Baker, Jr.
Huntsville, Tennessee
September, 2011

"I don't know if any of us can truly comprehend what it takes to create a museum from scratch, especially one with the breadth of the Museum of Appalachia. Few people have this gift, and John (Rice Irwin) is a pioneer in the preservation community."

Dr. Harold Closter
Director of Smithsonian Affairs
Smithsonian Institution
May 23, 2007

Elizabeth Irwin and husband John Rice Irwin teaching their grandchildren, Lindsey and John, how to sort and bag vegetables from the Museum garden.

Introduction

This book is largely in response to the often-asked question relative to who started the Museum of Appalachia and how it developed without any financial assistance, and totally without any knowledge of "museumology" on the part of John Rice Irwin, its founder and the author of this book.

During the years of the development and building of the Museum, my thoughts concerned only the practical and intrinsic aspects of collecting and displaying the artifacts, structures, and history of the area. As the Museum became known regionally, then nationally (and even internationally), I noted that more and more people became interested in the *how* and the *why* of the Museum—how one person, with no financial means and no knowledge of how to start or run a Museum, managed to put it all together. After a while I realized that "the story behind the story" is oft-times as interesting as the story itself.

The queries came from visitors from all fifty states and from some ninety-eight foreign countries. I believe I can state with certainty that these inquiries were from folks who were genuinely impressed with the Museum and who were appreciative of their time spent here at the Museum.

I had no stock answer to these questions, so the interest from these people started me to thinking—-why and how DID I start the project; and this book is a result of my meditation thereon.

As it turned out, the story of how the Museum came to be pretty much parallels my life story, since the two were so closely intertwined with one another. My autobiography on the one hand and the history of the Museum on the other are inherently inseparable. I would like to think that all this came about as a result of my love and admiration for the great old-time people of Appalachia, and my desire to portray them. It was they who were the catalysts for the creation of the Museum of Appalachia. Their interest in, and appreciation for, my goals encouraged them to provide their much-needed cooperation and assistance in myriad ways.

I have tried to remember that the purpose of the book is to exalt and to recognize the noble people of the Southern Appalachian Mountains by and through the Museum. The Museum stands as a useful tool in developing this portrait. My autobiographical inserts are likewise included only as they may contribute to the understanding of these peoples.

It should always be remembered that the Museum was possible only because of the cooperation, encouragement, love, and inspiration of these mountain folks of Southern Appalachia; to them we shall forever remain indebted.

John Rice Irwin, 2010
Museum of Appalachia
Founder and Developer

Chapter I
Life Among My Kinfolk
The Early Years (1930 – 1942)

All my people settled in a most beautiful and primitive area in the late 1700s—a place they named Big Valley. Some forty miles north of what would later become Knoxville, Tennessee, my kith and kin carved a niche in the wilderness.

In my growing-up years there was never any talk as to the origin of my ancestors—whether they were of English, Scottish, Scots-Irish, Welsh, or German, etc. The people in our region had pretty much been on the move for two hundred years or more, and their cultures had melded to the extent that any knowledge of ethnicity had long since been lost. It was many years later that I was able to assign my ancestors' origins to any European country. But it is safe to say that they, almost without exception, came from Northern and Central Europe. My mother's people, the Rices, are of Welsh ancestry, and some of them were among the earliest immigrants to come to America—as early as the 1600s. My four-times-great-grandfather, old Henry Rice, for example, was born in Virginia in 1717, and came, along with some of his fourteen children, to Big Valley in East Tennessee. He died and was buried in the Lost Creek section of Big Valley in 1818 at the age of 101. Many of his thousands of descendents later moved to Western Missouri, and thence to various places in the Midwest, and then on to Washington and Oregon, where many of his descendents prospered and raised large families.

The Irwins, whose ancestors have been traced back to the tenth century, were members of the Scottish royal families of the time, the earliest listed being William de Irwin, who was an armor-bearer for King Robert the Bruce. One of the first Irwins to come to East Tennessee and later to the Big Valley, about 1789, was Frank Irwin, who, with William Hancock, explored and first settled in the area. Among his descendents, and thusly distant cousins of mine, are General Carl Stiner, a local farm boy who became a four-star general in the United States Army and whose people came from the Big Valley clan, and the great American statesman, U.S. Senator Howard H. Baker, Jr., who was also descended from the Big Valley clan. According to research by Bill Irwin, the premier researcher and historian of the Irwin family, both General Stiner and Senator Baker are my fourth cousins. (Note: Both of these dignitaries are alive and well at the time of this writing, April 2010.)

The Weavers, Longmires, and Stooksburys are of English descent and also settled in the Big Valley area at an early date. Perhaps most surprising is the fact that many of my forebears who came to Big Valley were of German extraction, though they early on anglicized their names. For example, the Mullers became the Millers; the Scharps became the Sharps; the Schnatterlys became the Snodderlys; the Graffs became the Graves, etc. All these families, and others, became as one and no one claimed Scotch, English, Welsh, or German ancestry.

For the most part, when these families immigrated to America they migrated to Pennsylvania and Virginia. Some drifted down the Shenandoah Valley of Virginia, while others ventured into East Tennessee by way of North Carolina. Why and how they followed the footsteps of Frank Irwin and his compadre William Hancock and chose this beautiful, isolated area called the Big Valley remains unknown, but a study of the map shows that it was a forward progression of their southwesterly migration patterns.

They prospered there until 1935, when the United States government called upon them and many other adjacent families to leave their homes in preparation for the building of Norris Dam and its offspring, Norris Lake. Norris Dam was the first in a series of some fifty major and minor dams built by a federal agency that came to be known throughout the country as the Tennessee Valley Authority (TVA). The U.S. government's purchase of 152,000 acres for Norris Dam and Norris Lake required the relocation of 2,841 families and 5,226 graves, including the last refuge of my forebears. These families moved largely to the surrounding counties, few, if any, choosing to leave their familiar haunts of East Tennessee. Several of my kin merely moved as a group westward down the valley some twenty-five miles to the Robertsville community, and there the pocket of Big Valley folks lived peaceably and in harmony until 1942-43, when Uncle Sam's representatives once again rooted them from their homes for the building of Oak Ridge, Tennessee, a project which would become of national and international import, and one which would be known as the "Birthplace of Atomic Energy."

Grandpa and Granny Irwin is all my brother David and I ever called our adorable grandparents, but everyone else in the surrounding area always referred to them in a loving and respectable manner as Uncle John and Aunt Sara Jane. Although they owned a large, impressive Victorian home and had more than 300 acres of land, they always dressed and worked in typical farmer's work clothes. The one exception was on Sunday, when they sported their best attire. They are shown here after church at their home on a typical Sunday afternoon in Robertsville. (Photo by Ruth Rice Irwin, c. 1939).

After being relocated from the Big Valley homestead, my grandparents, Uncle John and Aunt Sarah Stooksbury Irwin, along with my father Glen Irwin and my mother Ruth and his brother Morrell, bought a large farm extending from the top of Pine Ridge to the south and reaching across the valley to the west, embracing some 325 acres.

My grandparents occupied a grand old Victorian-style house on the farm. It was on this farm that my brother David and I lived from 1935 until 1943. David was just thirteen months my junior and he soon caught up and surpassed me in size, prompting many people to think of us as twins. When I became old enough to attend school, my mother held me back a year so that David and I would be together in class. We continued together throughout high school, a fact that encouraged the perception we were twins.

My brother David, left, and I relax in Granny Irwin's back yard, c. 1936. (Photo by Ruth Irwin).

From my earliest recollections, I viewed the Robertsville farm as a source of wonderment. The unusually large barn stood obliquely between our house and the grandiose house where Granny and Grandpa lived. Cattle and mules ranged around the environs, chickens of a myriad mix roamed throughout the premises, and a drove of hogs enjoyed a large fenced-in pen. Apple, pear, cherry, plum, and peach trees provided a bounty of fruit for Granny's pies and for making jams, jellies, and preserves. She worked prodigiously, canning excess fruits and garden vegetables, which she stored in an underground cellar near her kitchen door.

My Grandmother Rice, at left, is shown here holding my
brother David; my Grandmother Irwin is holding me.
Grandpa Rice, left, and Grandpa Irwin, right, are in the
background. (Photo by Ruth Rice Irwin).

Even as a child, I viewed the homestead as idyllic, beautiful, and rustic. David and I never tired of exploring the back ridges, the freshets, and the creek which flowed through the acreage.

It has occurred to me that our lifestyle was little different from that of the Middle Ages. We were, in fact, almost self-sufficient. We raised, cut, and thrashed wheat, which we had ground into flour, enough for a year's supply. Daddy would permit David and me to make the all-day trip to the wheat mill in Lenoir City. We had to cross the Clinch River on a make-shift ferry, which was hand-powered, always a grand and exciting experience for us. Flour, unlike corn meal, will keep unrefrigerated for months, while corn meal becomes musty after a few weeks.

About every two weeks we would select and shuck the best ears of Hickory King corn in preparation for "going to the mill." There was one old water-powered corn mill at nearby Scarborough Community. It was an intriguing operation, the likes of which went back thousands of years.

We raised our hogs, and we butchered them around Thanksgiving each year. Mother would can the sausage, ribs, and tenderloins; Daddy would salt down the hams, shoulders, and side meat, preserving it for a year or more. Perhaps the most valued part of the hog was the rendered lard, which was obtained by cooking the meat skins until they had released all their fat. The residuals from the skins were called cracklings and could be sacked up and savored indefinitely.

After the hog was shot, scalded, and scraped of its hair, it was hung in a nearby tree by its hind legs held apart by means of a gambrel stick. Daddy would slit the animal carcass from the hind quarters to the neck and remove all the innards. The job David and I had was to hold the large galvanized wash tub to catch all the entrails. We observed and learned to identify the heart, lungs, kidneys, large and small intestines, etc.

One aspect of hog killings was repugnantly called "picking the guts." Mother, Granny Irwin, and several neighbors would take all the entrails down to the edge of the woods and pile them on a make-shift table where they would spend hours pulling the fat from the intestines. Two big kettles were kept hot and this intestinal fat was put into the boiling pots to render the all-important fat, or lard.

Granny would take what morsels she could salvage from the hog's head, feet, ears, tail, etc., and make souse meat from these. As was often said, the only part of the hog not used was the squeal. Any meat skins or scraps of the animal left over Granny used to make soap. The process was simple: She would pour water over hardwood ashes, the runoff being a lye-like substance; or she would use store-

Grandpa Rice came to our Robertsville home one week to cut firewood for Mother and he found this "mare & colt" in the limbs of a tree. He shaped them for David (left) and me; we were most pleased to have them, and we rode them for years. (Photo by Ruth Rice Irwin).

bought Red Seal lye. Mother would make lye soap, which she used for washing clothes. She always gave me the big chunks of soap for me to whittle into small slices which were put into a large cast-iron kettle for wash day. I would carve figures from the soap—one of which I named "Stupid in Hog Grease." I still have that piece of artwork somewhere.

We raised Irish potatoes, which we preserved in a little cellar beneath the threshing floor in the barn. It was a "common store house" and Mother and Granny would send David or me throughout the winter to get a mess of Irish potatoes. We also raised and preserved sweet potatoes, or yams. We made and canned kraut, and every kind of vegetable from the gardens.

One night about bedtime we heard a big ruckus out at Granny's chicken house and we all went out to investigate. We found that Granny's old dog Jack had bagged a 'possum in her hen house. I remember her saying "he's the rascal that's been catching my little chickens." When Uncle Morrell carried the 'possum out by its tail Granny said, "Where's your gun, Morrell? Get rid of that varmint before he gets away." It was at that time that I asked Granny if I could have the 'possum to sell to old Bill Key, the school bus driver. She agreed, but admonished me sternly not to "let him get away."

I put Mr. 'possum in a grass sack and placed it under a big wash tub for the night. I arose early the next morning and after our regular chores I changed into my clean overalls and was waiting for the school bus with my 'possum. When the bus arrived I proudly boarded the bus, 'possum and school books in hand (I was eight years old at the time). "What do you have in the sack, Johnny?" old Bill Key, the school bus driver, inquired. "I've got a 'possum to sell you," I replied. He felt it through the sack, following its backbone with his fingers. Finally he said, "Ah, Johnny, he is a mighty poor 'possum," and my exhilaration waned.

Old Bill continued, "I can give you six suckers and two candy bars, or 15 cents." I retorted, "Well, you can fatten him up a little with scraps before you eat him, and his hide would bring that much," but old Bill was unimpressed. I decided to take the 15 cents and I was somewhat consoled by the fact that it was all profit.

One of the few neighbors with which we had association was Lisha Miller, who, along with his wife and several children, lived in an abandoned chicken house on the adjoining Meek farm. He worked for my father occasionally for $1.00 for a 12-hour day, which was 25 cents above the going rate. He raised a little corn for Hal and Granny Meek on the shares. I remember a little field of corn that he raised across

the road from our house and that his wife would help him plow and hoe the corn in the mornings, and then she'd walk home about 11:00 to cook dinner. Lisha would roam the surrounding hills and streams in search of wild game for food. He sometimes went barefoot, and we often saw his tracks in the soft ground after extended rains. He would sometimes kill a squirrel, a rabbit, or a groundhog, but game was exceedingly scarce during those Depression years and his bounty was scant. I remember one time he passed by our house with two big mud turtles.

Sometimes Lisha would come to our house and visit for hours. He talked about his days in the "reform school" for fighting and nearly killing his adversary and how the wardens would strip them naked and whip them with blacksnake whips; and about the boy who drowned as he attempted to swim the Clinch River to escape.

When the first sign of unusual building activity occurred in our community, a railroad spur at Elza Gate, Lisha walked the seven miles to get a job and miraculously was hired. This was the first hint that the building of the great city of Oak Ridge was to occur there, and eventually tens of thousands of men and women were to be hired. Lisha walked the fourteen-mile round trip every day and became a trusted employee and remained employed by the government until his retirement several years later.

Even as a young tyke I abhorred not finishing a challenge. I recall one incident which I think illustrates this tenacious trait. Daddy, Uncle Morrell, and two or three hog buyers were in the process of "trading" but the buyers wanted the male hog castrated before closing the deal. Several of the men had tried unsuccessfully to catch and hold onto him and although I was only nine or ten years old, I decided that I could catch and hold the pig. I took some shelled corn and some tankage and poured it into the muddy lot, then the drove of hogs gathered ravenously around to eat it. Against my father's admonishment I got in the shoe-top high mud and grabbed the wily boar by both ears and he dragged me from one end of the lot to the other several times, covering me with a combination of mud and hog manure while Daddy and the other men were alternating between laughing and hollering for me to let him go before I got hurt; but I was determined to hold onto him. This went on for several minutes, the hog squealing and dragging me through all the slime. I knew that I couldn't hold onto him, but I never entertained the thought of letting him go free. Finally the totally exhausted hog stopped in his tracks and some of the men came to my rescue. Daddy came over with his razor-sharp Case knife and performed the "surgery" on the pig, and the traders bought him and the rest of the drove of swine. I had done what four or five grown men couldn't, or wouldn't, do; and I think they were impressed.

I always liked to be independent and pay my own way. My cousin Paul, who was a couple of years older than me, had an old and totally worn-out pair of shoes, and I bought them from him for a nickel, even though my mother and father always kept us in shoes. It felt good that I had bought them myself.

I've made reference to Hal and Granny Meek, whose farm adjoined ours. Although they owned a large farm, they were reputed to be extremely frugal. One day I saw old Hal stop his team of mules in the cornfield. He reached in his overall pocket and retrieved what I surmised to be a handful of home-grown tobacco with which he filled his pipe. Then from the bib of his overalls he took out a little "spy" glass and held it to the sun, aiming the resultant point of hot light into the bowl of his pipe. As he puffed, a hint of smoke arose, and finally, as he puffed, a larger plume developed. He had saved a match by so doing. (For five cents he could have bought a box of kitchen matches which contained 250 wooden matches, or 50 for one penny.)

There were two or three little one-room tenant houses on the Meek place that were ostensibly occupied by desperate and homeless people. One was occupied by a man who had the reputation of making moonshine. One day he was raided by the local sheriff and a couple of his deputies. After a footrace, they captured the ragged and muddy suspect, and for reasons I never quite knew, the sheriff stopped at the home of Grandpa and Grandma Irwin. There was a grand upping block there and we all went out to see what the commotion was all about. What I saw still lingers in my mind. They had captured the father of one of my schoolmates—unkempt, muddy from head to foot, and what appeared to me to be one of the most humiliated and pathetic men I ever saw. They had handcuffed him and brought him before us as witnesses that the sheriff and his folks were doing their jobs. Even as a child I felt sorry for this totally humiliated soul who was trying to make enough money to feed his family.

We knew that Granny Meek lived in the large imposing house which had once belonged, so legend has it, to the kin of the vice-president of the United States, John Nance "Cactus Jack" Garner. None of us had ever seen Granny Meek at the time. I suggested, and David agreed, that we take two chickens to Nash Copeland's store and buy some fruit and candy to take to her one Christmas morning. She came to the door and greeted us warmly, but didn't invite us inside. She seemed genuinely appreciative for the candy, oranges, nuts, etc., and we talked awkwardly with her for a minute. David and I were on the four-foot high porch and suddenly it occurred to me that the seat of my overalls revealed a bare bottom. I was more than hesitant to exit, which would require that I turn and expose myself. Hence, I decided to back off the porch, resulting in my "accidentally" stumbling off the porch backwards and falling into the boxwoods before making my retreat. This I did, much to the dismay and concern of Granny Meek, who asked, "Are you hurt? Are you all right?"

Even so, I remember this as one of our most memorable Christmases because I thought that we had genuinely contributed to Granny Meeks' Christmas—two little boys whom she really didn't know, taking the time and trouble to bring treats to her. Maybe the cliché is not without merit: "It is more blessed to give than to receive."

The preeminent enjoyment was when we explored these haunts with our venerable grandfather, whom we always called Grandpa Irwin, and who was known to everyone else as "Uncle John." He had been a farmer, but he was getting on in years when we, as children, knew him—a sort of gentleman farmer, in his seventies and eighties. He was a lay preacher and was often called upon to marry couples, preach funerals, and visit the sick and dying. Everyone, it seems, said Uncle John Irwin was the best man they ever knew. He never charged for his services, but sometimes the families would give him a dollar or two, especially if he had to travel a long distance to render his services (he never owned an automobile, nor learned to drive).

By the time David and I knew Grandpa, he often sat on the long veranda and read the newspaper and especially the Bible during the hot part of the day. He hoed in the garden in the cool of the early mornings and chopped stove wood in the late afternoon. Even on the hottest days, Granny kept a fire in her big kitchen cook stove, which consumed vast amounts of short sticks of "stove wood." I remember going with Grandpa down on the creek one day to cut a tree for stove wood, and he chose a large ash for that purpose. I later learned that the ash is an unusually hard wood, which produces a great amount of heat, yet it is easily split. I don't remember when I learned to identify every tree in the forest, or who taught me their names, but I think it was a combination of both of my grandfathers and my father.

Grandpa and Grandma Irwin (seated, center) and their children on a Sunday afternoon, after church. Seated, front row, left to right, are Lige Irwin, John and Sara Jane Irwin, Roger Irwin; back row, left to right, Uncle Morrell Irwin, Sophia Irwin Atkins, Glen Irwin (my father). (Photo by Ruth Rice Irwin, c. 1939).

Grandpa Irwin was born in 1861, the year of the start of the Civil War, and in his youth he knew people who could remember pioneer and frontier times and customs, even back to the era of the birth of the nation. He learned and passed on to David and me stories and traditions from his pioneer heritage. For example, he showed us the proper way to fell a tree with an axe and how to make it fall in the desired direction.

I remember one morning we struck out for the "back fields" with Grandpa and we wondered why he took along his cherished axe. When we neared the foot of Pine Mountain, we came upon a large cornfield where our father and Uncle Morrell were plowing the waist-high corn. The corn was dark green, rank, and tall, and had all the markings of a healthy crop except along the perimeter where the field abutted the forest. Here the corn stalks were small and spindly, and yellow and sickly looking. Grandpa pointed out that this was the result of their proximity to the large trees whose roots sucked the nourishment from the corn, and which also shaded it from needed sunlight. He proceeded to rectify the situation by girding the large trees adjacent to the

cornfield. He cut a small ring around the tree trunks, which would kill even the largest and most hardy oaks. This was the first (and last) time I observed the "deadening" of trees. This practice, so important in pioneer times, allowed the crops to grow rank and healthy. The dead trees could be harvested in the winter months for fence rails, fence posts, shingles, lumber, and firewood.

I remember one day Grandpa decided to take charge of one of those old plow mules and spell my father from plowing the corn. Every few steps the old mule would reach down and bite off the top from a large stalk of corn, although the mule was reined as high as was possible. She continued to destroy the stalks every few yards. Finally, in desperation, Grandpa asked David and me to hold reign on her while he went into the woods to cut a slippery elm sapling. He then peeled half-inch wide strips of bark from the elm. In the early spring the strong, tough bark was pliable and easily pulled. From these strips he made a bark muzzle, and that took care of old Maud's eating the corn stalks. After work he took this primitive but strong muzzle home, and for years it hung in the "gear" room at the barn.

On one of our treks to "the back of the place," Grandpa gave each of us what we commonly referred to as a "grass" sack, perhaps more properly called "burlap sacks." It was in the summer and we went to an old house near the foot of the ridge which we always referred as the "old Stringfield place," so named for the last family to have occupied the site.

We soon learned why Grandpa had us bring the sacks along. There were a few old apple trees from which we gathered horse apples, Limbertwigs, Rusty Coat, and other varieties. There was one heavily laden peach tree, called an Indian Peach. Its small, white-meated fruit had the most delectable, sweet, and juicy taste of any peach I've ever tasted (Hernando de Soto, the early Spanish explorer, had introduced the peaches to the Cherokee Indian in the sixteenth century, and the Indians planted orchards and came to rely heavily on the fruit, hence the name "Indian Peach.") When the first white settlers came to the region, they found numerous peach orchards, especially in and near the Cherokee villages in lower East Tennessee.

It was on one such trek with Grandpa that we were crossing a little branch when Grandpa called our attention to a small shrub-like tree, fully laden with encased nuts, and he said, "Now that's a hazelnut bush." As I recently recalled this trip, I called my brother David and asked him if he remembered our first introduction to the hazelnut nearly three-quarters of a century earlier. He did, indeed, remember this discovery, and even in more detail than I had recalled. He reminded me that subsequent to our first introduction to the hazelnut, we went every year thereafter to the little tree to harvest the tasty nuts. The memory of such a seemingly trivial event for such a lengthy period of time only underlines the power and importance of the time David and I spent with Grandpa. (I still have a small hazelnut bush here at the Museum.)

On one excursion with Grandpa up on Pine Ridge, we encountered a vine heavily laden with small grapes, which Grandpa identified as "possum grapes," and another grape vine with larger fruits he dubbed "fox grapes." There was also a somewhat larger wild grape he called "summer grape" but the biggest find of all was the wild Muscadine. The fruit of the Muscadine is much larger and one of the most delicious of all the wild grapes. Today there are domesticated varieties of the Muscadine, but these are not so large and plump and totally delicious as the wild Muscadine.

In the early fall we would sometimes go with Grandpa with our grass (burlap) bags to the high ridges on the westernmost part of our acreage to gather pine knots. These we found in profusion from the residual of large pine trees, which had totally decayed—except for the rich, resin knots. These were heavy with resin and would last, "they say," for more than a hundred years lying on the ground. We gathered these rich knots for kindling and they would burn for an extended period of time before they would be consumed. The rich resin would burn, but the knot itself would remain intact. Grandpa explained that this was the material used in making pine torches for lighting the pioneer cabins, and for night hunting, a practice which harkened back thousands of years. Grandpa would split these knots into fine splinters and place them in Granny's wood box behind her stove for starting fires. She used them parsimoniously.

When harvest time came in June, my father rented his cousin Conrad Stooksbury's wheat binder, a revolutionary farm machine that was invented in 1880 by Cyrus McCormick of the Shenandoah Valley region of Virginia, replacing the reaper he had invented c. the 1840s. The binder was somewhat cumbersome in cutting the wheat and oats from around the trees and in the fence rows, thus it left some of the grain uncut. That's when Grandpa got out the primitive hand-powered grain cradle and scythe, almost identical to the scythes used by the Egyptians for centuries before the birth of Christ to cut grain. He also introduced David and me to another ancient process: winnowing grain to clean away the chaff. I remember that he would toss the wheat and chaff from the loft of the barn on a windy day into a sheet which we held open on the ground. The light chaff was blown asunder and the heavier grains were caught in the sheet. Even then, when I was ten or eleven years old, I realized that we were replicating a method which had been used since Biblical times, separating the wheat from the chaff; and I remember the aromatic fragrance that exuded from the freshly-cut grain straw.

As we meandered through the meadows, along the creeks, and in the fields, Grandpa would point out various plants and their medicinal properties. He taught us how to make quail traps, and how to tap the maple trees in late winter, and how to boil the sap to make maple syrup and maple sugar.

I remember once that Grandpa commented on the Civil War. He pointed out that the Irwins were Southerners, but their sympathy lay mainly with the Union. He once said, "We had fought to establish the union and form a nation not so long ago, and we didn't want to see it split and destroyed," as would have been the case if the South had won the war. Because of this ambivalence, the Irwins stayed out of the fray, even to the extent of sometimes "hiding out" when the "recruiting" soldiers from either side came by searching for recruits. One exception was my great-grandfather, Elder Thomas Weaver, father of seventeen children, who served in the Union Army. Some of my forbears fought in the Revolutionary War and I am a member of the Sons of the Revolution. The local Anderson County, Tennessee, chapter bears my name.

Grandpa Irwin was one of fourteen children and several of his brothers would visit him in his elder years, and of course Granny Irwin would cook and wait on them while Grandpa talked and visited. All of his siblings were "good livers" except one—Shade Irwin. Shade never married and spent his elder years visiting and spending time with his kin. He would stay a few days, or sometimes a few weeks, with Grandpa and Granny Irwin. Grandpa would have him cutting and/or splitting stove wood, but mostly he would visit and talk. He was overweight, a diabetic, and not prone to do much manual labor, but Granny kept after him and she was able to get him to help Grandpa with the wood cutting.

My Granny Irwin was perhaps the most loving soul I've ever known. She had every right to feel put upon and to be resentful, but instead she was a most content, happy, and giving person. She was a bundle of love and she and I were in love with one another. She was one of two girls born into a family of eleven children. Her sister, several years older, married early and went to Oklahoma with her husband when Granny was a young girl. This left Granny and her mother to literally wait on the nine boys. The women cooked, sewed, washed, and did all the "women's" work for the family.

I was in Granny's kitchen one day and she was penning a letter to her "Sis" in Oklahoma while the pies were baking and she asked me how to spell "pie." That night I asked my mother why Granny couldn't spell simple words, and Mother told me that Granny's father would not allow her to attend school. He felt that the woman's work was in the house and gardens, and that book learning was unnecessary. This attitude was not a mean or cruel attitude on the part of my great-grandfather, but rather, a sign of the times, as it was a widely held attitude in those days and represented the status of men and women of that era. Granny later told me that as a young girl she would beg and cry to be allowed to attend the one-room school with her peers.

She was always up before daylight and worked until bedtime; I never saw her idle. But she loved keeping busy and always whistled while she worked.

She cooked for Grandpa and my Uncle Morrell, for all the field hands, and for frequent visitors. Grandpa would often invite the preacher and several friends and relatives home for dinner on Sundays. Someone counted more than twenty Sunday guests for the noon meal one time, and Granny always managed to provide—even if it required "two or more tables."

It is worthy of note that Granny had no electricity, no refrigeration, and no running water, and that she, with a little help from Grandpa, raised and canned all her vegetables. On Saturday afternoon she would capture David and me to go with her to the barnyard where she would point out to us the plump three-pound chickens which we were to catch. We would sometimes have to chase them for as long as half an hour, until they became so weak and fatigued that they would find a nook or cranny into which they would burrow their heads, much like the proverbial ostrich, in an effort to hide. Then it was just a matter of grabbing them. We repeated this until we caught all she needed for Sunday dinner—usually three or four. She would scald them in a bucket of boiling water after deftly wringing off their heads, then she would pluck the feathers (which she would save for pillows or feather bedding), and then she would singe the birds' pin feathers over an open flame before dressing them.

She always attended church on Sunday mornings before preparing her fabulous Sunday dinner—an array of fried chicken, country ham, potato salad, deviled eggs, pinto beans, green beans, fried okra, and pies, cakes, and much more. Often in mid-afternoon she would set up a "picnic" in the back yard for her six grandchildren.

When I was nine or ten years old, I would take my father's 16-guage shotgun and kill a quail or a dove, or a squirrel; and Granny would cook them for me with broth and gravy (my mother had an aversion to cooking any kind of wild meat). After I joined the Army years later and was serving in Germany, Granny wrote me often, though she was well into her eighties and had a limited vocabulary.

She seemed the epitome of happiness and contentment. She never took a vacation or attended a movie. Her joy came from giving to others, and from her association with the church. She was jolly and loved spending time with her many kinfolks who usually visited her and Grandpa on Sundays, often for the mid-day meal. The laughter and merriment was continuous and infectious, and her relatives seldom left without a gift of some sort from Granny—pies, cakes, preserves, a jar of pear butter, a can of cherries, or a mess or vegetables from her bountiful garden.

My brother David, on the right, and I wait for the bus on our first day of school in 1936.
Since I was only thirteen months older than he, my mother chose to hold me back for
one year so we could attend classes together. (Photo by our mother, Ruth Rice Irwin,
1936).

My brother David and I disembarked the Bill Key school bus a mile from our house; and on our way home we'd pull and eat a few turnips from the neighbors' gardens along the road (if it were in the fall or early winter). We'd also check for buckeyes from the banks of the little stream we crossed. When we got home we always changed clothes, carefully hanging our school overalls in a closet and donning our worn and tattered overalls. Mother would make sure that this was done properly. Next, we went "to do up our work." We'd carry corn to the vociferous hogs, and we fed the mules some hay and seven ears of corn each, if they had been working in the fields; otherwise we'd give them only three ears each. The chickens would steal enough of the grain from the hogs and mules for their subsistence, and, of course, they had foraged throughout the day. One of our primary after-school chores, however, was "hunting" the eggs.

My mother and Granny depended on egg money for whatever they needed from the weekly trip to Nash Copeland's store: to wit, pinto beans, baking powder and baking soda, salt, coffee, and bananas for the Sunday banana pudding. Quite often the hens would retreat far back under the floor of the house to make their nests and lay their eggs. After laying an egg they would fly out, cackling vociferously. Granny would spot them and after school she'd have me and David search in the shallow crawl space until we found the nest. Even then I dreaded the foot-high floor joists, but Granny persisted, directing us this way and that way until we found the nest of eggs. Even today, some seventy years later, I have nightmares about those claustrophobic experiences.

In the Depression years of the 1930s most farm families would sell their eggs to the store after culling some of them to fry for the family breakfast.

In the late 1930s eggs brought about 26 cents a dozen, and a good farm hand could be hired for 10 cents per hour, so Granny's "egg money" went a long way to supplement our livelihood, both in purchasing needed goods and hiring "help" for the farm. Our chickens and Granny's chickens foraged as a single and indistinguishable flock and if they laid eggs around Granny's house they were her eggs and those deposited near our house were Mother's eggs, and there was never any hint of dissension in the division thereof.

On Friday nights we would take the old coal oil lantern and "candle" the eggs to make sure that they were "somewhat" fresh. The age-old process of "candling" eggs consists of holding the egg up to a light source in a darkened room. By doing so, one could "see through" the egg and be able to detect problems related to the egg's "freshness."

In the summer, when the days were longer, our primary job was to "go get the cows" from the surrounding hills and drive them to the barn for milking. The family farm, as previously noted, consisted of well over 300 acres, ranging from the top of Pine Ridge on the south to the rolling knobs on the west. The herd of some forty Jersey cows knew their way to the barn but they depended on us to titillate them and drive them lazily to the milk barn. There was one old cow, more prolific than any of the others, which produced three or four gallons of milk a day. We called her "Old Fillchurn." Aside from her docility, she was impeded in her walk by her oversized udder. So we would catch her and ride her to the barnyard, and the other cows would follow.

Our father had an old hand-operated cream separator which separated the cream from the raw

Even when we were wee tykes, one of our daily chores was to find the herd of cows in the evening and drive them to the barn where Grandpa Irwin and Daddy would milk them. There was one old gentle cow named Fillchurn and David and I broke her so we could ride her in from the distant pastures. I'm in front and David behind. (Photo by Ruth Rice Irwin, c. 1939).

17

milk. He sold the cream to the Sugar Creek Creamery in Knoxville and the residual low-fat skimmed milk was fed to a drove of pigs and shoats. When they heard us coming with the milk cart, their raucous squealing could be heard for a mile. In addition to their diet of milk, we fed them corn and in the autumn we fed them pumpkins. When the shoats became fattened hogs of about 200 pounds, my father sold them to local "pen brokers" or took them to sell in the stockyards in Knoxville.

The small amount of cream we placed in little two-gallon cream cans two or three times a week. These cans were placed in front of our house for the "cream man" to pick up and take to the creamery. The creamery would send us a miniscule check every few days.

I once asked an old friend, Alex Stewart, if his venerable grandfather had much education and he answered by saying that his Grandpap "never went to school, but he had a pretty good education." I've often thought about the truism and meaning of this statement and how it seemed appropriate for my grandparents.

In addition to my elementary and high school days, I have a degree in history and economics from Lincoln Memorial University and a master's degree in international law from the University of Tennessee. I also have been awarded two Honorary Doctorate degrees and have completed one year of graduate work toward a PhD. degree.

But I can say truthfully that I believe that I learned more, and was more profoundly influenced by my four largely "uneducated" grandparents than by all of my schooling. As "proof" of this surmise, I point out my frequent mental references to them, my memory of them, and my scant, almost nil, recounting of that which I learned in my years of formal education. For example, I often say that never does a day go by that I don't think of something one of my grandparents said or did in reference to whatever subject was at hand. I'll reference them a bit later, individually, in this connection. But first I'll point out a trait held by all of them which may sound surprising, and somewhat shocking. As profound and deep as our mutual feeling and love toward one another was, they did not manifest this in any verbal or physical manner. I don't recall any of them ever saying "I love you," or embracing or hugging me. I asked my brother David about this, just to be sure of my recollection; and he readily agreed. But somehow we knew the deep and abiding love we had for one another. (The same is true with my mother and father.)

When I became eight years of age I was eligible to participate in the National 4-H Club farm program

(I didn't know until many years later that the 4-H Club was co-founded by the great-grandfather of my late daughter Karen's husband: T. A. "Dad" Erickson in Minnesota). David and I raised a few chickens as our "project" for the 4-H Club of America. We bought the day-old chicks and nurtured them to frying size and sold the chickens to Nash Copeland's General Store. We kept a record of the expenses in raising them until they were half grown and this was my first business enterprise. This was in the 1940s and all meat was strictly rationed for the war effort, so the demand was quite brisk.

It was about this time when we started picking blackberries in the back fields of our farm. It was a mile to the old pasture fields where the prolific blackberry vines grew and we would go there after the regular morning barn chores were completed. It would be noon by the time we filled our buckets with blackberries. After the noon meal, we would deliver the berries to our Aunt Sophie who lived over a mile from our place. All the walking jolted the heaped-up buckets and we would have to pick more berries along the way so that we could deliver a heaped-up measure as Grandpa Irwin had always admonished us to do.

Aunt Sophie and Uncle Frank paid us 25 cents per gallon, but the going rate at the time was only 20 cents a gallon. I was never sure whether they bought them for culinary reasons, or perhaps just to patronize their two nephews. At any rate, by the time we returned home it was time to do the evening chores. We had spent the entire day picking and delivering the berries, but that "quarter-coin" looked awful big and shiny and we were happy.

When I was about ten or eleven years old, I bought two 'possum hides from Lisha Miller. I remembered that a fur trader, Squire Hobe Brimer, would come by occasionally, buying animal fur and hides. Sure enough, he stopped by a few days later when we were grading tobacco and he asked if we had any "fur." I was exhilarated! I raced to the smoke house and brought the two 'possum hides and waited anxiously for him to make an offer. He tugged on the fur of the pelt to make sure the hair "wasn't slipping," and then he blew into the fur so he could better judge the texture. Then he said, "Possum hides are down this year and all I can pay is 15 to 20 cents apiece." My heart fell. And although I was a mere tyke of ten years, I had heard enough haggling to know that the first offer was not necessarily the final one. Timidly, I said, "I've got more than that in them. Could you go 30 cents apiece?" At this point my daddy and Uncle Morrell, who were there grading tobacco, laughed heartily, as did the fur buyer. How could the old fur trader not be amused, and then he said, "I can see that you're going to be a trader. I'll tell you the best I can do: 25 cents apiece."

I was pleased. I made 10 cents on the two and it was all profit. I was also pleased that my father did not intercede in his ten-year-old son's negotiations. I considered this to be a rare compliment from him.

It was about a year later, at age eleven, that I made my biggest and most profitable trade. I was with my daddy at the little barn on our farm and he and Uncle Morrell were trying to buy a cow from Powell Justice who lived in our rental house. I don't know why I remember seventy years later that it was raining and the rain on the tin roof hearkens back the melancholy of that dreary day. After my father and Powell concluded their negotiations I asked Powell about a pretty little heifer in a nearby stable. I boldly said to Powell, "How much would you take for that little calf?" and everyone laughed at my question. After it became apparent that I was serious, Powell said $25.00. Of course I didn't know its worth, but I knew that she was a beautiful calf and would someday make a good milk cow. Taking a cue from having listened to my father and others, I made a counter-offer. I said, "$15.00 cash money and that's all I can do. I'll give it to you for the calf." Powell said, "I can see that you're going to be a trader like your father. Let me see the cash and if it's $20.00 you have the calf." I agreed and became the proud owner of a fine heifer calf. My father tended to be critical of my negotiations, but he didn't interfere.

We took the young calf home and named her Minnie. My daddy didn't charge me anything for the hay and pasture she consumed. She was soon bred and he let me have the calf she had, which I sold for $8.00. She became a productive milk cow and I sold her later to my father for $65.00, the most profitable trade I'd made up to that time. He kept the productive milk cow for several years and she was considered to be one of the best in the herd.

World War II started in December of 1941 and soon the demand for scrap iron, tinfoil, etc., skyrocketed for "the war effort." David and I had an old red wagon which we pulled throughout our farm collecting worn-out plow points, broken pieces of iron, etc. Sometimes we'd go along the gravel roads in our area collecting any discarded pieces of metal. We'd also collect the tinfoil from chewing gum wrappers and especially the foil from cigarette packages. The "scrap iron man" would come by every few weeks and we'd sell to him (we'd roll the tin foil into balls and sell it by the pound—a scant amount as I recall).

In the fall of the year we'd gather walnuts as they matured and dropped to the ground. We'd then remove the outside hulls and sell the nuts at Bill Lockett's Country Store. He paid 9 cents for a heaped-up gallon and I added these pennies to my little bank, while David was more prone to buy candy and suckers with his money. We also bought and sold candy bars and garden seed and, as usual, Aunt Sophie and Uncle Frank were our major customers.

In the fall of 1942 and through the coming winter, the entire area which was to become Oak Ridge was vacated by order of the federal government. All the inhabitants were forced to move from every old homestead. Almost immediately a hoard of newcomers arrived and a city that had originally been planned for 13,000 people sprang, within a three-year period, from zero population to some 75,000.

Over the years these new settlers raised questions as to who lived there before they came: who settled the old hills and valleys, who tilled the land, who maintained the pastures, and what manner of people were they? And especially, they wondered about the methods and circumstances of the "overnight" removal of so many people. The following story relating to the above questions was, and is, intended to address some of these questions.

How It Was In "Oak Ridge" Before There Was an Oak Ridge

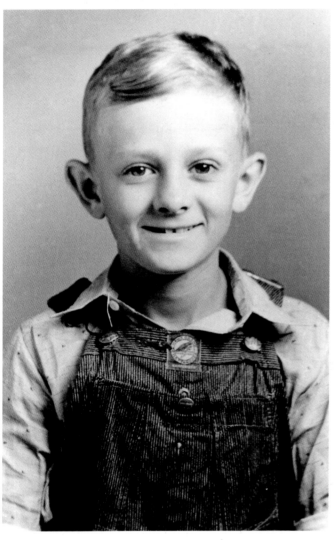

My mother was always concerned that my ears were too big, and she tried taping them closer to my head so they would grow properly. (Photo by Ruth Rice Irwin, c. third grade).

I was not quite twelve years old, but I knew something awful was about to happen. It was in the fall of 1942 when we heard that the Southern Railroad at Elza Gate had started building a spur line off their main track. There was not a town or village in that rural area on the Clinch River, a few miles below Clinton, Tennessee, and a railroad siding was a source of great wonderment in the valley.

It was about this time, October, I think, that the area was overrun with land surveyors. Some of our neighbors were notified by the federal authorities that their houses and farms were being purchased and some of them who had lived in what came to be known as "hot spots" were given only fourteen days to move. A letter dated November 11, 1942, and addressed to one Parlee Raby, was succinct and to the point:

> "The War Department intends to take possession of your farm December, 1942. It will be necessary for you to move, not later than that date."

No one knew how much land the government would need, and no one knew how many nor which families would be affected. Everyone speculated, and everyone hoped they would escape. Few did. An area consisting of about 56,000 acres was soon to be totally vacated.

The answer for our family came suddenly, stunningly. We returned late one Saturday afternoon from our weekly trip to McWayne's corn mill and Nash Copeland's store to find a notice tacked to our front door. I don't remember its precise wording, but I remember the essence of the message written on flimsy paper that fluttered and flapped in the chilly autumn breeze. I remember, too, the anguish on the faces of my father and mother as they read and reread the short message.

We had barns filled with hay, thousands of bushels of wheat and oats, and a sizable herd of cattle and numerous other farm animals. There was tobacco curing in the barns and corn not yet gathered from the fields. We had only a few days, the notice read, in which to gather up all our chattels and possessions and move from our Gamble Valley farm to a destination yet unknown (the government offered not a whit of assistance in helping us to relocate). There was no allowance for hardships, no exceptions, no provision for appeal or review.

Our farm contained the large, impressive Victorian home where my grandparents lived, two tenant houses, and a five-room frame house where my brother David and I lived with our parents, Glenn and Ruth Irwin. The government's offer was a total of $10,500 for the property in its entirety, including the barn AND the buildings, and of course the large home where my grandparents had lived. For this amount we soon found that we would be able to acquire only a fraction as many acres in the surrounding area, due partly to the inflated prices caused by the increased demands brought on by the multitudes of families seeking nearby farms.

Although those who owned a scrap of land experienced great hardships, those who owned no land at all, but lived as sharecroppers, had an even more challenging time when they were forced to move from what was to become Oak Ridge. I remember one such family who lived on our place. Bill and Lydia Wright had several children and literally lived from hand to mouth. Bill worked occasionally as a house painter, but had no other income. He was a sort of Jack of All Trades, but was often out of work, even at the rate of $1.00 per day.

On one occasion David and I wandered over to the tiny cabin where the Wright family lived. It was near suppertime and both David and I recollect to this day a portion of the worried conversation drifting from that little cabin. We heard Lydia, the mother, say to her brood, "There's a half-glass of milk left, who wants it?" And in a pathetic unison all the children begged in a chorus, "I do, Momma, I do."

Bill was the only neighbor in our community who owned a motorized vehicle, an old model A Ford which he had converted into a type of truck to haul his ladders and such for his painting jobs. He would scrounge from the dump large tires to fit over the threadbare ones that were on the vehicle.

It was a pathetic scene when the Wrights moved from their humble abode, and David and I happened to be there to see our playmates for the last time. Bedsteads, old chairs, baskets, cooking pots, and sundry other household chattels and accouterments were piled high on the hybrid "truck," and on the front and rear bumpers as well. Other extraneous items were loaded into a little two-wheel trailer of Bill's own conception. The little trailer was fully loaded with garden tools, mowing scythes, and the little black cook stove, the premier item for their new home, wherever it might be. And Bill's brother, old blind Doc, sat there resolutely holding onto the stove.

I stood there waving back at the passel of children, not knowing whether we would ever see them again. I heard that they were going down into Roane County, where Lydia's people were from, and that they would try and become tenant farmers (sharecroppers) in that area.

This sudden intrusion into our otherwise quiet and peaceful valley became the singular topic of conversation, and it burdened everyone, young and old, night and day. I remember not being able to sleep, wondering where we would go, and what it would be like never to see our classmates again, and how it would be to go to a new school where we would be total strangers. People couldn't decide whether to use the few days they had to gather their corn and grade their tobacco, or to look for a new home. Trucks for moving the families were next to

impossible to hire; and for those that were available it was difficult in those war years acquiring tires, repair parts, and especially fuel. All of these items were strictly and stringently rationed.

But the economic and technical problems inherent in such hurried-up moving, monumental as they were, did not compare to the mental trauma. One has to understand the cultural and ancestral roots to which rural folk become attached after a few generations, in order to understand the shock which results from uprooting.

My personal attachment to that Robertsville area home was deep and strong. There was not a foot of those three hundred acres that my brother David and I had not explored, mostly with our venerable grandfather. We had gathered wild salad greens along the meadows in the early spring, fished for the red-eye and buffalo in the creeks, and picked blackberries from the pastoral knobs near the old Stringfield place in mid-summer. We gathered hazelnuts, muscadines, and fox grapes in the fall, hunted rabbits in the winter snow and we tapped and spilled the sugar maple in February. Every day was an adventure and every field, hollow, ridge, and swimming hole was an old friend. It was inconceivable that we soon would be leaving, forever, these friendly haunts of our childhood.

But young folks could look forward to the future with enthusiastic optimism and they could quickly adjust. Old folks couldn't. They were, to some extent, living in the past, among the familiar hollows and ridges they had known all their lives. They were among their relatives and their neighbors and they, in their memories, lived among their ancestors as well. To leave this peaceful, friendly, and familiar valley and to take up new roots in a strange place, among strange people, was a prospect beyond that which could be imagined. It has been said that some of the old folks literally grieved themselves to death.

No one knew at the time that action by the government was to be swift and certain, and therefore efforts were commenced to thwart the move altogether. I remember hearing that there was to be a "big" meeting at the school house at Robertsville. Everyone was urged to attend and to the best of my memory almost everyone did. The word was spread that Congressman John Jennings would be there. I assumed that there was no higher, more powerful, and more influential person in the nation, except maybe the President. I think most of the people felt that way.

I have vivid recollections of that meeting. It was not unlike the testimonial services that I had witnessed in revival meetings at church and at the tent meetings. I especially remember one old white-haired woman who spoke in tones which wavered between anger and pathetic beseeching. Her great-grandfather was one of the first settlers there, she said, having brought his family and all his possessions from North Carolina in a cart drawn by oxen. She said he, along with all her people, lay in a little cemetery on their farm. And she said, "Four of my babies are there, too. We don't want to leave them."

An old man in faded and patched overalls took the floor and spoke. He said that he plowed the same fields, hunted the same woods, and fished the same streams as had his father, his grandfather, and his great-grandfather. His son, he continued, did most of the work on the old farm now, and his grandson would hopefully take it over some day. According to nature, he said, he didn't have much time left, and he just wanted to till his farm and spend his last days among his friends, neighbors, and relatives. He looked around the room with tears in his eyes, trying to think of a good way to end, and as he struggled for words, the entire audience broke into applause. The old man nodded awkwardly and sat down.

I don't know if Congressman Jennings knew the inevitability of the government's move to acquire the land from the people or not. If he did, he didn't advise them of the total futility of their pleas. As a matter of fact, the prevailing sentiment, as I assessed it, was that there was nothing beyond the scope of what a Congressman could do, and the expectation was that he could stop this governmental takeover of our land, our property, our community, and our lives. The meeting adjourned and a crowd gathered around the old legislator, pointing out how long they had known him and how fervently they had supported him in his elections. Small clusters of people gathered and wondered if the Congressman could stop the government from taking our land—some wondered if he really wanted to. Whether or not he petitioned the President to terminate the project, or to place it elsewhere, we never knew. What we did know was that the acquisition of the land moved forward with ever-increasing swiftness.

The surveyors converged on the entire area like flies after honey, and the drone of heavy equipment ripping the landscape apart was our constant companion. The apprehension grew as we wondered where we'd go, and how we could afford to buy another farm with the scant amount the government had offered us.

A few days ago, I found among my mother's papers a letter she had written to her own mother in this regard. It was dated November 24, 1942, just prior to our move. It read, in part:

"Some of the people are just about mad enough to kill over their prices (offered for their land). You remember the new house on up above Rogers on the left coming this way. It is built a lot like ours . . . on 80 acres of land. They offered them $3600 for the house and 80 acres and he (the owner) said his house cost him $5000. That is an example of what they're offering, so I guess we won't get anything. I wish this business was over with."

—Ruth (Rice Irwin)

In the meantime we worked literally night and day gathering corn, grading tobacco, sacking wheat and oats, and otherwise preparing for the prodigious move. My grandfather was a lay minister, and he believed in the strict observance of the Sabbath. But for the first time in his life, he consented to our working on Sundays. The ox was in the ditch.

My father bought another farm, the old Sam Hill place, about twenty miles up the valley, in the Glen Alpine community. The moving of all the crops, machinery, livestock, and generations of household items had to be accomplished by a single hired truck which broke down almost daily. It took dozens of trips and several weeks. At one point it occurred to my father that we had half of our possessions moved to the Sam Hill place, unlocked and unguarded. And while thievery and pillaging was not considered to be a problem in those days and in that area, the concern for security increased as more of our possessions were moved, and because strange workers poured into the area on a daily basis—to work at "The Manhattan Project." Late one afternoon, as Roy Edmondson's old truck was leaving our Robertsville farm piled high with lespedeza hay, my father instructed me to go with him and spend the night at the new place.

Uncle Frank and Aunt Sophia Atkins had moved nearby to a tiny temporary house, and I was to sleep there (on the floor) when I was not on guard duty at our house. I was to return to our Robertsville home in a couple of days.

But more loads of hay and corn came, then the cattle, hogs, mules, and chickens, and they all had to be cared for. After a while, the moving was almost completed, and I realized, suddenly and stunningly, that I would never return to that beautiful rolling farm home. Although I had not yet turned twelve years of age, I had been given the responsibility of not only guarding all the ancestral possessions, but of feeding and caring for the ever increasing number of swine, cattle, chickens, and even the work mules. Soon after my family came to join me, the area which was to become Oak Ridge, Tennessee, birthplace of

This was my seventh grade class at Scarboro School in the fall of 1942 when the United States Government ordered the school closed for the building of Oak Ridge. I am fifth from the right on the front row (seated) and my brother David is located on the right end of the second row.

atomic energy, was closed to visitors and the tightest security was put in place.

Years passed and a city of some 75,000 people was built on land which our family and others had vacated. When I finally did return as a young man, I found nothing of the tranquil and nostalgic countryside of my childhood. Great plants had been built, one of which, known as K-25, was said to have contained the largest floor space of any building in the world.

Then in 1970, some thirty years after we left our old home, I was appointed Executive Director of the Tennessee Appalachia Educational Cooperative, whose offices were in Oak Ridge almost in sight of a portion of our old home place. But when I reflected back on those happy and carefree childhood days, spent roaming through the lush meadows and over the familiar hills, I never thought of them as being nearby. They were far away and long ago in my mind, and their physical closeness did nothing to change that.

I sometimes saw boys exploring the old knobs where David and I trudged every summer afternoon in search of the milk cows. I am reminded of the buckeyes we found on the streams, the papaws and horse apples we gathered, and the rabbit tobacco we chewed along the way. I wondered if those boys now roaming those old fields and meandering streams enjoyed themselves as much, and loved the land as intensely as we did. I wondered, too, if they ever

wondered what that land and those hills were like before their time—before their grandparents came there in the early 1940s, just as we were leaving.

Aunt Sophia and Uncle Frank Atkins. (Picture taken by Ruth Irwin, c. 1944).

23

Chapter II

My Growing Up Years on the Mountain Road

1943–1949

As noted earlier, our family was forced to leave the Robertsville area for the building of the massive Oak Ridge project. I was so attached to that beautiful, pastoral and bucolic farm that it was devastating to realize that I would never again see those environs. My distress was eased somewhat when my father bought a 130-acre farm from his cousin, Sam Hill, some twenty miles "up the valley" near where my forebears had settled in the late 1700s. The farm was located in the Norris area on the Mountain Road, and David and I soon began to explore it thoroughly—the wide valley, John's Creek, and Lone Mountain, in the community known as Glen Alpine.

My father, Glen Irwin, on his way from the milk barn to the house on Mountain Road, one mile southeast of the Museum. (Photo by David Irwin, c. 1970s).

The house on the new place was a rough wood-framed five-room structure that had never been painted. The wooden shingled roof leaked badly and mother put no less than a dozen pots and pans in the attic to catch the rainwater. We soon discovered that 'possums lived there, eating our sweet potatoes and partaking of the plenteous water supply. We even found an occasional snake in the downstairs closets.

There was only a small fireplace in the living room, and no heat in the bedrooms. I remember how warm and snug I was between two feather beds and under seven quilts one cold night. It was eight degrees above zero in the bedroom when I awakened that morning.

Our water supply was an outside, hand-dug cistern which was fed by the rainwater from the roof of the house. This served all our water needs, including our drinking and cooking water. One summer we decided to "clean out" the cistern and when we removed the water there was nearly two feet of black muck in the bottom. Soon thereafter my father hired a well-digger to drill for water, which he struck at some 150 feet. This was a joyous day for my mother.

There came a time, about 1943, when the old house was almost uninhabitable and my father contracted with one of Sam Hill's sons to build a new five-room house. They left the second floor totally unfinished, with no floors nor ceilings. David and I, using old hand-made wooden tools, took it as our task to finish this area, with the expert help of Grandpa Rice. When finished, it became the bedroom for David and me, and it remained so until I left home in 1949.

It was here that I lived with my parents from 1942 until 1949 when I graduated from high school—a little lifetime, I thought, of exciting and romantic endeavors. Those were busy and productive years.

Granny Irwin proudly poses with her seven Irwin grandchildren, all boys. On the front row, from the left, are Jimmy, baby Johnny, John Rice (holding the baby), Paul, Tommy, and David; on the back row are Rex, John Earl, and Granny Irwin.

I visited Grandpa and Granny Irwin less frequently, although their new home was only two miles away. We also had close relatives nearby. On the south side of our farm was my father's Uncle Eli and Aunt Mary Jane Stooksbury, and to the east were my father's sister Sophia and her husband Frank. We soon became acquainted with several neighbors there on the Mountain Road and it was here that I spent my growing-up years, from the time I was in the seventh grade until I graduated from high school.

David and I attended Glen Alpine Grammar School, held in an old building constructed in 1914. The toilet facility was a little, unenclosed, "four-holer" outside structure, and I remember the stench and the lack of any privacy. The boys would gather around it at recess to smoke and visit. They would roll their cigarettes from the loose tobacco from Prince Albert cans and as soon as they lighted their cigarettes, some "less fortunate" boys would holler out, "I get ducks," and then someone else would say, "I get second ducks," and so on. By the time second ducks became available the cigarette was a half-inch long, but long enough for the ten-year-olds to get a few puffs.

The sixth and seventh grade classes were held in one large room where the teacher, Ruth Longmire, presided. The room was heated by one large coal-burning stove in the corner of the room, and the well-behaved boys were rewarded by being given permission to go to the basement and get a bucket of coal, or to dust the erasers in the school yard on a large cedar tree.

One day, Uncle Frank drove his little black coupe to the schoolhouse to take David and me home. He said our father had lifted a heavy log and had become ill, resulting in what was later diagnosed as a heart attack. For several months he was unable to carry on with the farm chores, and David and I took over the entire farming operation that spring and summer. This included the care and milking of the cows; the mowing, raking and stacking of the hay; the planting, cultivating, and harvesting of the tobacco and corn; as well as the planting and cultivating of the gardens. On occasion we hired a cousin, Amos Stooksbury, to assist us; but we knew what to do and how to do it, and we managed quite well, considering that we were only twelve and thirteen years old respectively. All the mowing, raking, and hauling of hay was done with a team of mules which we learned to drive and handle expertly—or so I thought. Our father's strength slowly improved and by the next summer he was able to resume his normal activities on the farm.

In the summer of 1943 we had a prolonged drought and the pastures dried to a crisp. It was so dry that Uncle Eli would go to the woods every morning and cut saplings and even larger trees for his little herd of cattle. They ravenously devoured the foliage—a diet which they ordinarily would not have eaten.

All of our pasture was gone, and it was unlikely that the fields in the large meadow were going to produce any hay; so Daddy decided to turn the cows loose in the would-be hay fields. In the fields adjacent to the large meadow, we were growing corn, with no partition fence. This required constant vigilance to keep the hungry herd away from the corn fields, and it became my job that summer to herd the cows and to keep them in the hay fields and down on John's Creek where they could graze on the willows, weeds, and other vegetation.

This job was most relaxing and enjoyable. I envisioned myself as a cowboy from the Old West. I watched the mother groundhog bring her four young ones out in morning and show them the red clover blooms which grew near the water's edge. She would stand upright and on guard while the young feasted on the blossoms, oblivious to any danger. I caught the runt of the litter and took him home as a pet for a few weeks, and then I decided it would be happier with the brood and took him back to the den.

I watched the crows and studied their system of always posting a look-out whenever the others were foraging in the corn field; and I watched the bluebirds come and go to their nest in a hole in a hollow sycamore tree. There was not a structure in sight and there was no sign of civilization except the cleared fields and the crops. And I thought the life of a herdsman would be a good one, albeit a lonely one. It provided time to meditate and think. One day the little groundhog that I had returned to its den strayed too far from its burrow and old Tom, my hound, caught him and quickly made waste of him. One minute he was a beautiful, active creature and the next minute he was a limp and lifeless ball of bloody fur, and I was greatly saddened.

This all happened before we started the dairy, and our herd consisted of stock cattle, mostly Hereford, generally referred to as "White-Faced." My father sold them in late summer and agreed to deliver them some few miles away. In order to save the cost of trucking them to the new owner, my father decided to drive them. Here again, I imagined that we were back in the Old West on a cattle drive. But the excitement soon waned and exhaustion took over. I learned early in my life that there is an art to driving cattle, a technique that some of our helpers seemed not to understand. We drove the herd down the gravel Mountain Road, fording Hind's Creek, and

to their destination without difficulty—my first and only cattle drive.

During the war years of the early 1940s, most foodstuffs were stringently rationed at the stores, and this boded well for David and me and our chicken business. We bought the chicks when they were two or three days old and fed them until they weighed two or three pounds, then Uncle Frank would take David and me to Clinton where we went door-to-door peddling them.

It was no less than amazing that we could sell live frying chickens to the housewives, many of whom had never before killed and dressed a chicken. Uncle Frank would park his little coupe and David and I would hold a chicken under each arm and I would go down one side of the street and David would take the other side. In some cases we would have to behead the chickens in order to make a sale. I recall knocking on several doors one day, but no one was buying. It was a cold day, and I looked down at the birds, cuddled under my arms, and they had become so cozy that they had closed their eyes and looked sleepy and sickly. It was then that I started shaking them rather vigorously before approaching each house. We sold the live fryers for $1.00 to $1.25 each, and this was when farm laborers could be hired for $1.00 per day, so a working man could only buy one chicken for a full day's work. During the Great Depression hired farm hands would often be given a single hen for a 10-hour day's work.

I was no doubt strongly influenced by our neighbors on Mountain Road in the Glen Alpine Community. Uncle Eli Stooksbury, my Grandmother Irwin's brother, was our closest neighbor, and he and Aunt Mary Jane owned the farm adjoining ours. Eli was a small, wiry man who was always jovial and happy and whom I loved to be around. He and Aunt Mary Jane reared five girls and one son. Uncle Eli had never had a regular job, except tending the little farm. Like most of our neighbors, he never owned any means of transportation—not even a buggy or a riding horse. He kept a few cows and occasionally he sold a calf, and Aunt Mary Jane and I kept a few free-range chickens for their eggs. To this day, I wonder how they managed to raise a fine family on such a scant income. He and Aunt Mary Jane raised a garden and she dried and canned its bounty, and they gathered and preserved wild edibles, such as blackberries. When Uncle Eli killed a squirrel, Aunt Mary Jane would stew it and make gravy for the family. Uncle Eli would tan its hide, using wood ashes, and he cut the hide into narrow strips, which he used for shoe strings. He also used the strong strips to mend the harness for his mule, Little Joe.

As parsimonious as he was, Uncle Eli was always at the fore in helping his neighbors in time of need.

I used to help him put up his scant crop of hay for Little Joe and his half-dozen head of livestock. He had a patch of woodland which he was always clearing to provide a little more area for grass for his livestock. Most people would slash and burn, but not Uncle Eli. He would cut a cedar sapling and use the trunk for fence posts. Then he would cut all the limbs for Aunt Mary Jane's cook stove. He even used Little Joe to pull out the stump, which he would split for the fireplace. He loved his little place and he took good care of his few hillside areas.

Uncle Eli had no way of knowing that he would indirectly contribute to the enjoyment of untold thousands, even millions, of people. He made a simplistic musical "instrument" he called a mouth-bow, or music bow. It was not unlike the bow used by the Indians for hunting and warfare. He used hand-rived cedar for the bow itself, and for the string he used a strand of wire from the front porch screen door. He would place one end of the bow at the edge of his mouth and when he plucked the string, in a similar fashion as when playing the Jew's harp, he could produce a unique sound. The novelty of the instrument, and its unique musical tune, was always a crowd pleaser. Of course he never had a crowd to please, but his son Carlock, after he returned from the war, did. Years later, Carlock became, and remains, a mainstay at the Museum of Appalachia and a member of the Museum of Appalachia Band. I introduced him to the eminent Archie Campbell, a principal in the founding of the enormously popular "Hee-Haw" television program; Archie took Carlock to Nashville, where he appeared on the nationally televised show, ostensibly before an audience of some thirty million people. The response was so great that he appeared a second time. Carlock also appeared in several TV documentaries at the Museum and played with the Museum Band for some forty years. Among those who enjoyed his mouth-bowing art were senators, governors, Hollywood producers, and such notables as Oprah Winfrey, Jane Fonda, and Brooke Shields. All of this emanated from the little ninety-eight-pound farmer, Uncle Eli, who passed on this unique gift to his son. Carlock's mouth-bow playing was especially popular in later years at our annual Museum of Appalachia Tennessee Fall Homecoming.

I, along with a few neighbors, was at Uncle Eli's house the night he died. I remember when they carried his lifeless body down to the waiting hearse, and I remember seeing his white hair blowing in the wind; I experienced a great feeling of sadness.

Uncle Frank's farm joined ours to the east, and I worked for him occasionally in his garden and in his tobacco and corn patches. He was too old and feeble to do much work, and one year he leased the tobacco allotment to me and I tended and harvested the acreage "on the halves."

One summer, Frank hired my two cousins, Earl and Paul, along with David and me, to chop the weeds from his corn field. At the end of a long day we went to Frank's front yard where he was sitting, to "settle up." He paid each of the other boys 50 cents for the day's work, and when he came to me he said, "Now Rice, you've been wanting that little hand-cranked coffee grinder for a long time, and I'll either give it to you for the day's work or I'll give you the 50 cents, like I paid the other boys." I readily took the antique coffee mill and the other boys chided and laughed at me for my poor choice. For 50 cents I could have bought a goodly amount of candy and Cokes at Nash Copeland's store, but what good was an obsolete coffee grinder?

I'm often asked why and how I started collecting for the Museum, and what item I first acquired. Certainly, this coffee mill was one of the first family pieces I acquired, at the age of fourteen years. It reminded me of the ones my grandparents used on early mornings before breakfast, and the subsequent and pleasing aroma it produced.

Uncle Campbell and Aunt Ella Sharp had the next farm, extending from the valley floor to the top of Lone Mountain. One day old Tom, my hound, actually treed a big groundhog in a mulberry tree, laden with ripe mulberries. (Few people, I've learned, believe groundhogs can climb trees, but there he was, twenty feet off the ground, feasting on the sweet fruit.)

When I finally got the groundhog dislodged from his perch, Old Tom made the most of him. I knew that my mother, being adverse to cooking wild game, would not cook him for me, so I took him to Uncle Campbell. We skinned it, Aunt Ella cooked it, and we had a sumptuous meal of groundhog the next day. But that's not the end of the story. We buried the thick hide in wood ashes and kept it moist for three days to loosen the hair, which began the "tanning" process. Then we coated the hide with corn meal and "worked" the pliable hide, twisting and wringing it off and on for a couple of days. Then Uncle Campbell beat it over a cedar tree repeatedly. When the process was complete, the hide was "tanned" and was rendered supple and pliable.

Uncle Campbell then carefully split the pelt in two equal parts—one half for me and one half for himself, enough for several pairs of shoe strings. When

Uncle Campbell died several years later I attended the little country auction, and among the chattels I bought was a wooden box of his own making which contained sundry items. At the bottom was his portion of the groundhog hide, which he never got around to using. Like so many of the pioneer stock, Campbell was warm, gentle, and accommodating, while being as tough as nails.

When he was in his prime, he fell from the uppermost framing of a barn he was helping to build in Big Valley, striking his back on a stump as he landed. His wound became seriously infected and the local "doctors," who had never attended medical school, informed him that only an operation could save his life. He consented to the surgery, but only if it could be performed in his home. The doctors were most reluctant to undertake such serious surgery under such primitive conditions. Here is the story, as Campbell told it to me: "They didn't want to cut me open at my home, on the kitchen table, so I told them that I'd do the cutting from my belly side if they'd show me where and how, and they finally agreed to do the cutting themselves. I got four of the strongest men in the neighborhood, one for each limb, and they cut me open and drained the infected area. In a few weeks it all came back (the infection) and I got the same two doctors and the same stout men to hold me down. But the problem came back again for the third time and it was harvest time, and I hated to call the men back; so I decided I could go through a third operation without being held down. I took hold of the legs of the table and told them to cut away, and they did. I didn't have any pain killer, not even a dram of whiskey, but I managed to stand it." Campbell had three massive scars in his abdomen as a reminder of the ordeal.

Campbell was the epitome of saving and thriftiness. I visited him late one afternoon and he was feeding corn to his pigs. He had a five-foot-long stick, a hoe handle, I think, and he had a sharp knife attached to the end of the stick and was jabbing the snouts of the pigs with this knife to keep them from rooting up the ground. A more common and humane practice was attaching copper rings to their snouts; but each of these rings cost a fraction of a penny, and Campbell's method cost nothing.

So, Uncle Campbell was parsimonious, but not at all selfish. He would walk down to our place and sometimes spend an entire day helping shock hay or grade tobacco, and, of course, never charged anything.

Polk Irwin, a distant cousin, owned several hundred acres just above Campbell's place and he was reputed to be the hardest-working man in the valley. When Polk was only fourteen years old, he and a brother left home for Illinois where he started working as a field hand for $8.00 per month, plus his board. He reportedly worked there for fourteen years, saving 98 percent of his earnings. (He was devastated when his brother drowned while swimming a river near where they worked.)

After working in Illinois for those several years, he came home at the behest of his mother and bought his father's farm. When the tract of land that would later encompass the entire town of Norris was put up for public auction, Polk was one of the two people who bought it. He worked literally night and day, and acquired additional land in the Andersonville-Norris area. His land and his farms were recognized by the Tennessee Valley Authority as models of exemplary agricultural practices, and were selected as models for demonstration purposes for visitors. As a result, TVA brought visitors from many foreign countries to study how old "worn-out" land could be made productive again.

Polk married Sarah Elizabeth "Lizzie" Heatherly on January 19, 1915. After he and his bride moved into a small log cabin where Polk's father had raised his ten children, Polk built a comfortable five-room house for his wife and only child, Juanita Irwin Crosby. The total cost of the house was $200, part of which was paid for with a cow and a mule. He cut and sawed the trees for much of the lumber.

Not long after Polk had moved back to Tennessee, he was summoned by a neighbor, Ike Graham, to come to see him. Ike and his wife had twelve or thirteen children, and Ike's wife had died recently, and Ike himself was on his death bed. Ike beseeched Polk to care for his large family after he was gone. Ike died shortly thereafter and Polk and Lizzy took care of all these children until they were able to place them with local families.

I worked for Polk some as a teenager, especially during wheat harvest time, and, although he demanded much in the way of relentless labor, he paid well.

In the fall of 1942, I became interested in trapping (and hunting) fur-bearing animals, an avocation which I pursued actively throughout my high school years. I had three trap lines. One was on Buffalo Creek, mainly for muskrats; one was on John's Creek, where I concentrated on mink and muskrats; and the third was on Lone Mountain, where my quarry was mainly skunks and 'possums. These were the late Depression years, and most farmers trapped a little to supplement their modest income, resulting in a scarcity of all fur-bearing animals.

Photos of the author as a teenager, from his scrap book.
(Taken by his mother, Ruth Irwin, in the 1940s).

Photos of the author as a teenager, from his scrap book.
(Taken by his mother, Ruth Irwin, in the 1940s).

Every morning I would run the trap lines long before daylight, early enough to get back to the old log barn to help David and my father milk and feed the cows—all this before the beginning of the school day. I had a problem with skinning the skunks because the lingering odor could not be washed off my hands after the skinning process. I contracted with Uncle Campbell to skin most of the skunks and stretch the hides on boards made for the purpose. I paid him 10 cents for each skunk he skinned and stretched.

I remember one day when school was cancelled because of the cold weather. The highest Fahrenheit temperature reading that day was eight degrees above zero, but I, despite my mother's protestation, persisted in running the John's Creek trap line. The one catch of the day was a skunk at a point where a gushing spring emptied into John's Creek. The creek was frozen solid except for where the spring water emptied into the larger creek, so I decided to skin the skunk before it became frozen stiff. I would skin a while and the carcass would freeze; then I held it in the spring water a few minutes and continued skinning the skunk until it again froze; and then back into the spring water. Of course my fingers would become numb from the cold. It took me at least two hours to finish the task. That was the sole catch of the day, and the skunk hide brought only 35 cents. Oftentimes I would not catch anything. These austere times would often come to mind when I was spending money to equip the Museum.

Once I went into partnership with a neighbor boy who was my age. I was to do the trapping and he was to do the skinning and we were to divide equally the receipts from the hides. Over a week's period I caught 4 skunks, but my partner never got around to skinning them and they were beginning to rot, so I went ahead and skinned them in their half-decomposed state. In an endeavor to be fair, I gave him half the proceeds, but that was the end of the partnership arrangement. I believe they brought 60 cents each. (I learned early on to be careful in choosing partners.) Brother David never developed any interest in hunting and trapping and there were no boys my age nearby to accompany me on my hunting and trapping forays.

We had a little dog that somehow acquired the name Victory. This was in the early days of World War II and the prefix "Victory" was assigned to myriad things—Victory gardens, Victory scrap-iron drives, Victory suppers, etc. Victory was a smart and feisty little dog and I started hunting with her at night—always by myself. The only light I had was the common kerosene lantern, which produced only a

pittance of illumination. One night I was back in the knobs near the foot of Lone Mountain when Victory started barking vociferously and I soon discovered that she had bayed a skunk. She was circling it as she yelped excitedly, and I noticed that the skunk was inching its way toward a large ravine, entangled with vines, saplings, and brush, and likely the site of the skunk's den. I didn't have my trusted .22 rifle with me and I knew that I'd have to act quickly if I were to capture the quarry. I saw a long cedar root which made a suitable club and went after him. I was only twelve at the time, but I recalled hearing the older boys (and men) say that if one struck a skunk on his back it would cause paralysis and disable it from spraying its repugnant liquid. This I tried and when I did so the skunk responded with a more than liberal dousing of the foul defense concoction on me—from head to toe. The good news was that I was able to bag the skunk and the bad news turned out to be disastrous.

I put him in the burlap sack and started home and the stench was almost unbearable, but miraculously the smell became markedly less offensive after a while, as is often the case when one's sense of smell is lessened and even deadened after a period of time. At first I feared to go home, lest my mother would not let me into the house. But alas, I fell upon a plan.

I stopped by Aunt Sophia and Uncle Frank's house to test the extent of the offensive odor. Aunt Sophia had totally lost her sense of smell from a childhood disease but I thought I could depend on Uncle Frank, notwithstanding that he was a prankster of the first order.

I put the sack containing the skunk on their porch and went inside. I asked Uncle Frank if he could smell anything and he held his head back and sniffed and sniffed and finally he said, "No, I don't smell nothing." He later said that the odor was totally stifling and that he could hardly keep from gagging.

So, based on my clearance from Uncle Frank, I proceeded on to our house, only a few hundred yards away. I no sooner opened the front door to my house than I heard my mother's feet hit the floor from her bed. "Don't you dare come in this house," she said. "You'll ruin everything we've got. Stay on the porch and I'll throw you a clean shirt and a pair of overalls."

Uncle Frank laughed and chuckled over this incident for years to come, but he and I became close, and since he was childless he became a second father to me. We'd sit in his front yard late in the afternoon, just before sundown, and look at the majestic Cumberland Mountains in the distance. We'd talk about Daniel Boone and the early settlers who passed through Cumberland Gap and how times were in those pioneer days.

The trapping season opened on November 15, as I recall, and ended in early February. Fur hides were only usable during these winter months. When I was about thirteen or fourteen I partnered with an old neighbor, Elmer Sherwood, and he and I became fast friends. When I started the Museum of Appalachia years later, he was the first person I hired to assist me. He was well steeped in the ways of pioneer and rural life. We would set traps over a two- or three-mile stretch and he could remember where each one was located. He taught me much about not only trapping, but all aspects of the woods and streams, and about the ways of the old people.

One of my most successful winter catches was when I was fifteen years old. I had about thirty-five or forty good pelts which I had stretched, cured, and hung safely, I thought, from the rafters of our old blacksmith's shop. I shipped pelts occasionally to F. C. Taylor Fur Company in St. Louis and sometimes to Sears, Roebuck Company in Chicago. But this particular year I had planned to sell the raw hides to Tom Melton, an old fiddler and fur buyer. A few days before he was to arrive I caught a 'possum and went to the blacksmith shop to add it to the lot. But to my great surprise and distress, I found that something had almost totally destroyed my season's work. The villain, a cat I thought, had scratched, clawed, and chewed the pelts almost beyond recognition. I was devastated; all those early mornings, the weekends—all for naught. I can hardly describe my despair. There were two or three weeks left in the trapping season and I tried to replenish the loss, but with little success.

Among the hides I had lost was a much-valued mink skin. I was considered to be the first of the local trappers in the neighborhood to actually catch a mink and it was the goal of everyone who dabbled in trapping to catch one. The news that I had bagged one had spread throughout the little Glen Alpine Community. The mink is strictly a nocturnal animal and I had never even seen the wary animal. As far as I knew, none of my neighbors had either. We had begun to wonder if they even existed at all in our region. We had only their occasional ill-defined tracks in the mud as evidence. They frequented John's Creek and Buffalo Creek, and I had studied the form of mink tracks from an old fur trapper's magazine and learned to identify them. I had never in my life been as excited as when I caught that first mink and I ran all the way home to show it to David and my parents.

Once, while running my trap line on Buffalo Creek, I fell through the ice and almost drowned. This had happened to me once before when the ice on our pond gave way and I miraculously escaped there also.

After running the trap lines in the pre-dawn day I was back at the log barn to help my father and David feed the stock and milk my share of the cows—some eight or so. After the milking, David and I would roll a little two-wheeled hand cart down to a big spring to get the evening milk which we had deposited into the cold spring water the night before. Then my father would take the morning milk and the milk from the previous evening to Norris Creamery and unload it. Although it was a half-mile from the creamery to the high school, Daddy would put us off at the creamery and we walked from there to the school in order to save the precious gasoline.

Although my father would have readily paid for my 25-cent school lunch, I chose to wash dishes in return for the noon meal. I was soon promoted to be in charge of the cash register for all those who ate in the cafeteria.

When I was a sophomore, my teacher entered me in the local speech contest. When I was awarded first place, he entered me into the regional contest in Knoxville. I did a great deal of research in preparation for this event, but I contracted a pretty serious flu-like symptom, which resulted in my being bedfast in the days preceding the contest. My mother begged me to give up entering the event, but I would sit before the big fireplace and work on the speech as long as I could each day and then go back to bed. My subject was "A History of the Federal Farm Price Systems," a rather complicated and controversial program. When the day came for the big event, I thought I was adequately prepared and I caught the local bus to Knoxville. While I felt absolutely prepared for the event, to my utter dismay I earned only second place.

When the contest was over, I realized I had missed the bus to Norris. We had no telephone at home and it was near dark, and I knew my mother would be worried. In my frenzy, I hired a taxi to bring me home, costing more than the small fee I received for second place in the contest. Everybody said that this was the first time a taxi had ever been on the Mountain Road and the locals chided me for "riding home in such style."

When I was a junior, I was elected by popular vote as president of the high school student body and presided at certain meetings involving that body.

Hunting and trapping became a passion for me, starting when I was in junior high school and continuing through high school. (Photo taken in our front yard in the Glen Alpine community near Norris, Tennessee).

David and I took classes in agriculture and shop under the tutelage of our teacher, Robert Weems. He always referred to us as his favorite students. I was active in the Future Farmers of America (FFA) organization and one year I organized what we then called an "Amateur Program" where I invited local and regional musicians and other entertainment acts to perform. I offered prizes for the winners and the second-place award was $15.00, which was won by a group from nearby Union County. One of the members of this band was Carl Smith, who was later described, along with Hank Williams, Sr., as ushering in the "honky tonk" sound in country music. When I was in the Army in Europe a few years later, Carl's music had gained national notoriety and was regularly heard, not only in this country, but in parts of Europe as well. Whenever I heard his music being played in Europe, I remembered that his share from the show I sponsored here was a mere $5.00. He gave me credit for helping him start his illustrious career.

One lazy Sunday afternoon I decided to go to the old Rice Gristmill located on a popular tourist route a few hundred yards below the famous Norris Dam. The water-powered wooden mill, featuring hand-carved white oak cogs and wooden gears, was built in the Big Valley by James Rice, my great-great-great-grandfather, in 1798. The old mill was moved to its present location when the valley was flooded, and was now under the auspices of the State of Tennessee as a part of the Norris Dam State Park. It was featured and pictured for many years in the *World Book Encyclopedia*. I walked to this quaint old mill some five miles from our home and found

Grandpa Rice stands beside the old Rice Gristmill his great-grandfather built in 1798 on Lost Creek. (Photo taken by his daughter, Ruth Rice Irwin, c. 1946).

several out-of-state visitors there, marveling at the ingenuity of this ancient relic; but there was nothing there to indicate its background, nor its history. That was when I was inspired to write a pamphlet on the subject.

I visited a few relatives, gathering pictures and information; and in 1948, when I was a junior in high school, I published the pamphlet, "*A History of Rice's Old Mill*," which was sold at the mill for 25 cents each. It sold well—some fifty to sixty copies per day—and when I occasionally visited the mill on the weekends I was kept busy autographing the modest publication. It eventually went into its thirtieth printing.

An old gentleman named Joe Rankin was the curator for the mill at the time and he always introduced me as a descendent of the builder and touted me liberally. It was largely through his promotion that the booklet sold so well. One morning Joe drove his old A-Model Ford to the Mill and parked it in the usual place, and then killed himself with a pistol he always carried with him for protection. I was greatly shocked and deeply saddened when I received the news.

There was an old man who lived out on the Norris Freeway and he sold minnows to the fishermen for bait; and he contracted with David and me to buy the minnows from us. We seined extensively in John's Creek for the little fishes. One day we were on a rather large sandbar, just above a waist-deep pool, when a large water snake swam downstream, headed for the large swimming hole, no doubt its habitat. My first reaction was to climb the steep bank to provide him passage, but I became entangled in the brambles and stumbled back to the sandbar just as the writhing snake was passing through. I remember the horror of stepping on it with my bare feet and I remember the snake striking my heel before I could move away. It got a good lick on me and cut two large gashes in my heel. These water snakes were considered to be non-poisonous, and we continued to seine for minnows. I never reported this incident to my mother, lest she would restrict our seining and swimming in the creek.

I have always had an inclination to not relent or abandon any project I started—a trait that I attribute largely to my forebears and to our culture. My cousin, Allen Longmire, for example, often tells of my encounter with a muskrat. I had long forgotten the incident, but Allen's version is as follows: I was with David and my cousins Earl and Paul down on Buffalo Creek when we saw a large muskrat swimming downstream, a most rare sight in midday, since it is a nocturnal varmint. I immediately

jumped in the creek, expecting to catch him by his neck, forgetting that there is effectively no neck to a muskrat, i.e., the head is effectively connected to the shoulder portion of the animal. No sooner had I grabbed him than the muskrat grabbed hold of my thumb. Neither the muskrat nor I relinquished and his rodent-like incisors sank through my thumb nail and then he pierced the underside of my thumb, biting bone deep, and giving no signs of letting up. I, on the other hand, gave no thought to letting go of his pseudo-neck. My compatriots finally pried the rodent loose and we bagged a fine pelt—our only catch of the day. I bear the scar to this day.

I was always looking for better places to trap and it occurred to me that Bull Run Creek (a redundancy often used in our region), which bordered the farm of my Grandpa and Grandma Rice, might offer such an opportunity. I gathered some forty traps and went there for a three- or four-day stay with my venerable grandparents. My relatives and compatriots at home were aware of this venture, and everyone was anxious to hear the outcome. I spent the first day, from twilight to dark, setting the traps, without even a break for the noon meal. The next morning I was on the trap line at the first streak of day and at dusk that evening I dragged myself back to my grandparents' home with not a single catch. They were more disappointed about the dismal result than I was, I think. The second day and the third day were equally disappointing, although I did catch a single small raccoon.

When I returned home, my folks, as well as the neighborhood friends were eager to hear of my "great success" and of all the pelts that I had collected. I was totally embarrassed and even humiliated to have to report the total failure. I later learned that this section of Bull Run Creek had been totally "trapped out" by the local farmers and hunters.

The experience of my Bull Run Creek fiasco could have been infinitely worse—even disastrous. I was working my way down the creek bed a few feet below the level of the meadows when I stepped on a two-foot high ledge. When I did, my head was level with the adjoining fields, and there stood a hunter with a shotgun cocked and pointed directly at my head. I was wearing a fur-type cap and the hunter had mistaken it for a fur-bearing animal. He was so shaken that he had to sit down. He had come within a few seconds of killing me, and he was totally mortified to the point of being speechless and of course I was equally mortified.

Our high school years in the mid-1940s witnessed the tail end of the old-time medicine shows. I think it was the middle of that decade that an old entertainer and promoter by the name of Bob Drake brought his act to the nearby village of Andersonville. He called the show "Goldie West and the Sun Valley Boys." After the day's work was done and the cows were fed and milked, the local farmers and neighbors would gather down at Mon George's Store to sit and listen to the music and singing and to hear Bob and Goldie extol the virtue of the herbal medicine that would cure everything from snake bites to rheumatism and lumbago. I liked the old-time music and I decided I wanted to learn to play the fiddle and the guitar. I had already heard and been imbued by our local hero, Fiddlin' Bob Cox. Bob Drake and Bob Cox inspired me not only to learn to play the instruments, but eventually to form my own band.

In 1945, I think, I bought a Stella guitar from my cousin, Amos Stooksbury, for $4.00. Not only did I not know any chords, but I had no idea how to tune the guitar; so I took it over to Bob Cox's cabin, where Bob tuned it and showed me how to make two or three chords. Bobby George and I practiced many hours into the late afternoons, and on the weekends.

It was also about this time, when I was fourteen years old, that I bought a fiddle from my Aunt Maggie Butcher. I heard that she had it for sale for $15 in Knoxville, and I talked my father into driving me over to buy it from her, which I did from money which I had saved from my trapping activities. I practiced in the late afternoon, after supper, but I was not a quick learner.

In the shank of the evenings I would sit on our front porch and practice, and "serenade" our neighbors. But honesty compels me to admit that I could never get the hang of the noting and bowing, and I decided that I might do better with a guitar. I bought a harmonica and practiced playing it as I went after the cows in the back knobs each evening.

This elemental exposure to these instruments did result in the band I later formed, and we played for community gatherings throughout the region and eventually we played at the Museum for groups from throughout much of the world.

I bought this fiddle from Uncle Fate Butcher and tried mightily to become a good fiddler, but I failed miserably. Then I bought a Stella guitar from my cousin, Amos Stooksbury, for $4.00 and learned to play in local groups. All the while, I was practicing on the harmonica, even as I drove the cattle home for milking. I later bought a mandolin from a West Virginia soldier while I was stationed in Germany. Although by no standard was I an accomplished musician, I did form an old-time country band and played in more than one hundred shows in the East Tennessee region and surrounding states, and even played for the Tennessee State Legislature. (Photo by Ruth Rice Irwin).

Chapter III

More Motivation and Inspiration from
Grandpa and Granny Rice

Granny Weaver Rice, at right, with her class of students—remarkably, more than half of these students were her brothers and sisters, of which she had sixteen. (Photo from a family album).

Although I talked quite extensively about Grandpa and Granny Irwin in the first chapter of this book, I mentioned only in passing Grandpa and Granny Rice. But this in no way should infer their lack of influence on me. Grandfather and Grandmother Rice lived only twenty winding road miles from our home. We visited them only every few weeks, and David and I would sometimes spend a few days with them. I was impressed by them from my earliest memories, and this exultation grew over the years. In fact, my first book, *Marcellus Moss Rice and His Big Valley Kinsmen*, was a biography of Grandpa Rice. I regretfully and inexcusably admit that I pretty much ignored Grandma Rice in the book about my grandfather. But I'll try and make amends here.

Granny Rice was the oldest child of Saloma and Thomas Weaver, and as such, she pretty much assumed the role of matriarch of her fifteen siblings. Her father was an Elder in the foot-washing Primitive Baptist Church. In this capacity he traveled, by horseback, rather widely throughout East Tennessee, and he was often gone for days at a time.

Granny Rice was somewhat stern, the executive-administrative type, even when engaged in neighborly and charitable endeavors. She would have excelled mightily, I think, in the business world, had she had the opportunity to do so.

Grandpa was the quiet and patient and gentle soul—a prodigious worker totally full of history, and an adamant disciple of everything historical. He, like my grandmother, came from old East Tennessee pioneer stock, and their similar, as well as their divergent, characteristics enabled them to carve a most bucolic home place on Bull Run Creek, some twenty miles north of Knoxville.

Grandpa remembered that he and Granny first met when they were each five years of age. Although they saw one another only on rare occasions, somehow it became understood that they would some day marry. On a rainy day in January 1904, they drove themselves in a horse-drawn buggy to a nearby preacher to get married, and they found the old minister sitting on his front porch. He suggested that they stay seated in the buggy because of the

Grandpa Rice and Granny Rice by the stone wall they built at their apple orchard at their home. (Photo by Ruth Rice).

weather, and he stood on the porch and performed the short wedding ceremony.

On rare occasions Granny Rice would spend a few days with us, mainly to help Mother when she was not well. Granny kept constantly busy and when she was caught up with the housework she would help in the garden and with the milking. She not only kept busy herself, but she made sure that everyone else around her was kept occupied as well. When David and I would come in from the fields with Daddy for the noon meal, dead tired, we were accustomed to taking a short twenty-minute nap before returning to the fields—but not when Granny Rice was there. She would always have some beans for us to break, some peas to shell, or apples to peel "while we rested."

Her large yard was literally filled with potted flowers and plants—a hundred or more, it was said—and she and Grandpa carefully cared for them throughout the summer and until the danger from frost was imminent. Then the plants would be carried to the basement for the winter. The cuttings and young plants had been given to her by her relatives and neighbors and Granny knew the origin of each one. In turn, she would give young plants to her kith and kin.

David and I have often wondered how our grandparents managed to create such a beautiful estate with virtually no income. Granny had taught school until she was thirty years old in a one-room schoolhouse, where her brothers and sisters constituted more than half her student body. Grandpa had served in the Spanish American War and had worked as a day laborer out West.

From these efforts, I'm sure they saved most of their meager wages—enough to buy a few acres of unimproved land on Bull Run Creek, adjacent to Granny's father, Elder Thomas Weaver. They cut and saved enough timber to build a beautiful ten-room house. They planed the lumber by hand and applied a "permanent" slate roof. They likewise built the largest and most attractive and utilitarian barn in the region, with a self-supporting roof patterned after the design of the Mormon Tabernacle, which Grandpa had visited in Salt Lake City.

They eventually bought two adjoining tracts of land. They installed a carbide lighting system for the house, and had one of the first indoor bathrooms in the community. Grandpa bought a small hydraulic ram water pump which pumped water to the house and barn from the spring at the foot of the hill. The pump ran for some sixty years without any maintenance or fuel cost.

They, in later years, bought a car, but neither ever learned to drive. A neighbor, Grant Graves, on rare occasions, would drive them to the mill or to the store in nearby Halls Crossroads, and sometimes

Grandpa and Granny Rice are shown here with the nearly finished barn they built, in large part with their own hands, on their homeplace on Bull Run Creek. The design was inspired by the Mormon Tabernacle, with its totally self-supporting roof, which Grandpa visited c. 1900. Grandpa is shown at the apex of this self-supporting barn, and Granny is shown on the ground, just to the right of the door. Grandpa would extend a rope to the ground, Granny would tie it to a timber, and then Grandpa would pull it to the top.

The house Grandpa and Granny Rice built with their own hands on Bull Run Creek, c. 1905. Soon after they were married in 1904, Grandpa and Grandma Rice, with the help of one man, cut timber from their woodland, hauled it to the sawmill, and dressed the lumber for this impressive house. They built in a secluded area surrounded by mountains and Bull Run Creek. The house featured lightning rods and a slate roof; a little more than a year was required to build it. The children in the photo are unidentified. (Photo by Ruth Rice Irwin).

over to visit us. As a teenager I would drive Granny to visit her numerous kin, mostly nieces and nephews (more than a hundred of them).

Prior to our making these trips she would have Grandpa and me load the car with vegetables, fruit, berries, flower cuttings, and such to give to her relatives and neighbors along the way.

From their gardens, grape arbor, and orchards they produced practically all their food, both for winter and summer. They canned beets, kraut, and bushels of beans; and they grew enough Irish potatoes, sweet potatoes, turnips, and cabbage to last throughout the winter. They canned grape juice, blackberries, strawberries, goose berries, and even made their own vinegar from apple peelings and apple cores. They kept cows for milk, butter, buttermilk, and cheese. They saved chicken feathers for pillows and feather beds. They kept ducks and a small gaggle of geese down on the creek for their eggs, but most especially for their feathers, which

they traded to the peddlers for various needed items through the ancient system of barter.

They raised broom corn from which the broom straw for their brooms was made. I remember as a teenager taking Granny to an old blind man over on Tazewell Pike who made brooms for a portion of the broom straw Granny took to him. No money changed hands. The same barter system was employed with regards to the milling of corn. The miller charged one-eighth of the grain for grinding the corn, which was a one-gallon charge for a bushel of corn.

In earlier years, Granny wove enough rag rugs for her entire house, and she made most of the clothing for the family. I cannot think of one single piece of furniture in the entire ten-room house that was not handmade. A few fine pieces, mostly beds, were made by Granny's father, Elder Thomas Weaver, and Grandpa Rice made all the other pieces. He also made some of the sparse furniture for our modest house, after Mother and Daddy were married.

Grandpa Marcellus Rice is shown here by the water wheel of the old Rice Mill built by his great grandfather James Rice in 1789. Pictured, from left, are his two grandsons, David and me (the author), and Granny Rice. In back, behind David and I, are his daughters Ruth Rice Irwin and Ruby Rice Little.

Grandpa and Granny had 100 acres of timberland and Grandpa would cut enough trees to make all the lumber needed for various purposes on the farm. I remember when I was a small tyke helping Grandpa load the logs onto the old horse-drawn wagon and taking them to Fred Martin's mill to be sawed into lumber. We drove down the little gravel road beside a high and rugged cliff on one side of the road and a mountain stream on the other side. I was impressed with the isolated, primitive, and beautiful scenery alongside the lonely road. Even then I realized that this trip could have been the same as it would have been hundreds, or even thousands, of years ago: a gentle and venerable old man with his ten-year-old grandson, the docile team of horses, and a load of logs. I felt the love Grandpa had for me and perceived

the pleasure he seemed to have in being with me.

As Grandpa cut the timber in what they called "The Hurricane Tract," he was always on the lookout for three- and four-forked pronged limbs suitable for making stools for Granny's flower stands. He also saved the tree laps for the kitchen stove and for the fireplace.

I liked to sit around the open fire in the winter evenings to watch and listen to the hissing of the sap from the ends of the freshly cut oak, and to smell the fragrance of the burning lichen and moss on the bark. I especially liked to listen to Grandpa tell stories of his fascinating life.

Among the few store-bought ("brought-on") items, especially during the Christmas season, were oranges. We would peel and eat them, and Granny and Grandpa would place the peelings on the hearth to dry. The following morning they would be dry and crisp and made excellent fine kindling. They had an oil-like residue and would burn as if soaked in kerosene. We would place them, sparingly, in the coals left from the previous evening, and they would immediately burst into flame. This would save both matches and heart pine splinters, and the orange peel aroma was most pleasing.

I was visiting once with the great musician and entertainer, John Hartford, in his home in Nashville, Tennessee, and we were eating oranges before an open fire. I told John about how my grandfather used to save the peel from the oranges for starting the morning fire. He later told me that he started drying the orange peels to kindle the morning fires and to smell the rich aroma produced by this practice.

Granny had an old and faded ice sign which she would hang on her front door when she knew David and I would be visiting, indication to the "ice man" how much ice she wanted for the purpose of making ice cream, usually 25 cents worth. We used the wooden hand-cranked freezer, and after loading the freezer with the ice cream mixture we would always put a small amount of salt into the ice that we packed around the freezer to make the ice colder. One day I noticed that Grandpa saved the water from the melted ice and I wondered why. I soon learned. He took the bucket of salty water to the barn loft and poured it on the loose hay so the cattle would find the hay to be more palatable. It saved buying the required salt for the livestock; it also helped to control the dust. Again, they wasted nothing.

One cold morning I went with Grandpa to his long woodshed where he kept myriad poles and saplings for firewood. He was cutting the smaller ones for the stove, only fourteen inches or so in length. It was cloudy and blustery that morning and random flakes of snow were blowing in the wind. Grandpa never missed an hour's work because of the weather and I could see that he was not suffering from the inclemency. Conversely, he could see that I was getting cold, although I kept busy neatly stacking the stove wood. I believe that I was no more than five or seven years old. Grandpa finally said, "Rice, why don't you go to the house and help Granny? It's getting mighty cold out here." Although the offer was tempting, I turned down the invitation. I enjoyed doing "a man's work" with Grandpa.

A few minutes later Grandpa said, "I believe it's getting colder—let's go to the house and warm." As we did so he gave me a stack of sticks to carry, and I noticed that he carried a three-foot-long log, some twelve inches in diameter. He carried this sourwood

This is the little sourwood wagon Grandpa Rice made for me, using only a saw and a hammer. Today it occupies a proud place in the Hall of Fame at the Museum.

log to the fireplace, along with a saw and hammer. Then he said, "We'll make you a little wagon so you can haul more firewood." He cut off four two-inch thick "wheels" and he worked, with my "help," throughout the day and well into the night on my wagon. It wasn't just a plaything; it replicated in every respect a large horse-drawn wagon. He made the rocking bolster, the hounds, the coupling pole, tongue, and all the other parts of a traditional farm wagon. The following morning this marvelous wagon was finished and sitting in the living room, and I was excited and pleased beyond words. Grandpa was already out cutting stove wood and I proudly pulled my little wagon to the woodshed and started hauling stove wood to Granny's kitchen. The fact that I could put it to a utilitarian use was as pleasing to me as the wagon itself. Maybe Grandpa knew this all along.

Many years later, when I was in the process of gathering items to start the Museum, I thought of this handsome little wagon, and I wondered what had happened to it, and I asked my mother. "The last time I remember seeing it," she said, "was out there under the floor of the old smoke house, pretty much falling apart."

I was able to retrieve the pieces from much debris and clutter and put it together, and it is now proudly and prominently displayed in the Museum. In the meantime, it has been featured in movie documentaries, nationally distributed newspapers and magazines, articles including the once nationally popular Foxfire publications, *The Smithsonian*, and *The National Geographic*, to mention a few. I'm just regretful that Grandpa didn't live to see the little wagon become so famous.

Once I accompanied my grandmother to Washington to visit her oldest daughter, Ruby, who worked for the government. (Ruby was subsequently chosen for membership in "Who's Who of American Women.") As we started to leave for this trip, my grandparents suddenly discovered that I was wearing a little red cap, and they immediately concluded that it should be replaced by a hat. Granny went to one of the upstairs rooms where my grandfather had discarded his ancient felts with the wide brims and after a while she returned beaming triumphantly because she had succeeded in saving the day by finding the quaint old hat.

I stood there before the fire with my light blue suit that I had proudly bought with twelve dollars of my trapping money, and eyed the operation with growing suspicion. The hat was placed upon my head by Grandma with as much pride as if it were a crown; and when she removed her hands, it fell to my ears, and I stood there barely able to see. "Now," I thought, "this will put an end to the hat business," but it didn't. They were not to be outdone.

"Give me a paper, Dad," Grandma demanded. And straightaway my grandfather returned with an issue of *The Knoxville Journal.* I think they stuffed the whole sixteen pages behind the sweat band, and when I tried it on again it fit "perfectly," or so they decided. But in the last-minute preparations, I managed to "forget" the hat and took instead my little red cap. Granny lamented half the way to Washington that I had been so careless.

Any time my grandfather's name came up where neighbors or kinfolk gathered, someone would invariably say, "Sill Rice is the hardest working man in the county," and the same could have been said for Granny. Sometimes I would help him haul hay during the summer. He was the only person I ever knew who worked all aspects of cutting, mowing, raking, and hauling the hay with no help. He was in the hayfield at the first signs of light and he worked until dark, about 9:00 p.m. in the summer. And if it were a moonlit night he would return after supper and work far into the night. I remember sitting on the front porch one night with Granny listening to the katydids and talking, and we decided that we'd stay up until Grandpa came in. We waited on him until near midnight and we finally went to bed. The next morning, at 4:30 a.m., I awakened to the aroma of coffee being brewed and I knew Grandpa was up and stirring. Work to my grandparents was not drudgery, but something they relished and enjoyed.

I suppose one of the reasons I was so enamored with Grandpa Rice was the romantic and adventurous life he had experienced during his younger days. As we sat around the proverbial hearth shelling peas, breaking beans, peeling fruit, and the like, Grandpa told of his adventures. Grandpa's greatest desire was to own a little piece of land, no matter how poor it was.

Grandpa talked about when he was a teenager, logging in the Cumberland Mountains near Lake City, Tennessee, some forty miles from his home, for $15.00 a month. He and his partner, Kige Weaver, slept in a little dirt-floored shack and did their own cooking of meals that consisted mostly of potatoes and green apples. He told me about going to work in the coal mines with his brother-in-law, Robert Hankins, when he was fifteen years old and he reflected on all the hazards they beheld.

It was customary in these mines for each miner, along with one "buddy," to have his own "room." He would start digging a small hole off a main artery of a mine and for years work back into the mountain. When Grandpa joined his brother-in-law, they had gone three miles back into the four-foot high shaft where they worked for twelve hours a day. A wooden track extended the entire distance for a small wooden car which, upon being filled, would be pulled out of the mountain by a small mule. The roof was supported by an occasional vertical timber, which held the mountain from the miner's head. At the end of this long narrow passage lay the two miners on the cold damp slate, digging relentlessly into the rich vein of coal. Black powder was a useful expedient, but it did not eliminate the strenuous labor. It is impossible for anyone to appreciate the plight of the miner unless he has visited him at his work, far from the light of day. The long, narrow passage which connects him with the outside world, and with life, is sometimes no more than four feet in height, and even then it is supported only by twisting, splintering timbers.

The miner, with the help of the buddy and his mule, could make as much as $5.00 in a ten-hour workday, but this was unusual. Since the mountain was honeycombed with dozens of such burrows, the danger of a slate fall-in was always extremely imminent, and hundreds of miners were trapped or crushed far under the mighty Cumberland Mountains with no wife or mother to give comfort. In one mine disaster alone in Anderson County nearly 200 miners perished.

Later on, Grandpa went to Missouri to work as a

Coal was transported directly from the mines to local customers "in the valley" in mule-drawn wagons. Grandpa Rice worked in the mines for a short period of time as a young man.

day laborer, trying to make enough money to buy a piece of land. "I didn't care about how poor and steep it was, I just wanted to have it for my own."

Although he had several relatives in western Missouri, he was not able to get a job when he went there in the late 1890s. He worked for three months for his cousin, Frank Rice, without pay, except for his room and board. He was such a good worker that his cousin started paying him three cents per bushel for gathering corn, in weather so cold that his feet became frostbitten, a malady which bothered him for the rest of his life. After several months working for various farmers in eastern Missouri for $15.00 a month, Grandpa received a letter from his mother saying that his father was on his death bed, and begging him to come home, "... if you want to see your father again."

He did go home, in 1895, but not in time to see his father alive. He stayed at home and made a crop for his mother and his sisters. After the corn was gathered the neighbors had a corn shucking for the Rice family, an event to which more than forty friends and relatives came. His next foray was to travel to Illinois, where he worked for $15.00 a month, always saving every penny for the little piece of land he and Granny yearned to buy. He returned from "the West" and volunteered for the Army during the Spanish-American War, during which time he served in Puerto Rico helping to protect the native population. After he was mustered out of the Army, he returned home briefly; then, in 1901, he went to the Oklahoma Territory where he participated unsuccessfully in the drawing for a piece of land.

Grandpa's experiences in Oklahoma, and later in Missouri, were filled with excitement and adventure for me, a ten-year-old tyke, and I never tired of hearing him tell and retell about the time he worked for David Masterson, the second cousin of Bat Masterson and Jesse James' neighbor. He worked for Thomas Bruce on a farm adjoining Jesse James' mother's farm. Bruce's wife told him about her infamous five outlaw brothers, known as "The Dalton Gang." The Dalton gang was shot and killed in a raid in Coffeyville, Kansas. He also recalled digging for Jesse James' gold where it was ostensibly buried on Thomas Bruce's farm.

He told about talking with people who knew Jesse James and how the Pinkerton detectives "blew off" Jesse's mother's arm while trying to capture him. He talked of how she plowed the corn fields with her one good arm. He told the story of how Bob Ford shot Jesse in the back, and how Ford himself had later been murdered. How could I NOT have been titillated by the romantic tales of the old West?

He told also of the murder of his older cousin, Henry Snodderly, and his wife, Serena Clear Snodderly, and of the subsequent hanging of the two murderers near Grandpa's home in Maynardville, the county seat of Union County. It was the day before Christmas in 1894 and the Sheriff brought John Stanley and his younger companion, Clarence Cox, to the gallows in a wagon pulled by a team of horses. They stopped the wagon just a few feet from the platform and asked the two condemned men if they had any last words. Stanley made a little talk. He said, "Boys, I hope none of you ever comes to this. It was drinking and gambling and running with a wild crowd that has brought us here today. I'm responsible for the Cox boy being here, and I beg you to spare his life." Although the old man pleaded for the Cox boy's life, his sentence had already been given by the judge and jury and the local sheriff had to obey the verdict.

"The old man," Grandpa said, "took a twist of tobacco from his pocket and bit off a big chew, and he said, 'I have no more use for this tobacco, boys,' and he offered it to anyone who wanted it, and some old man came up from the crowd and took it and thanked him."

Someone standing near my twenty-one-year-old grandfather said, "See that old man over there with a wagon and a team of mules? That's the daddy of the Cox boy and he's brought his wagon and team and a coffin to take his boy's body home." A few minutes later both men were dangling from the make-shift scaffold in full view of a crowd of several hundred people.

Private Marcellus Moss Rice in his Spanish-American War uniform, c. 1898.

I don't know how much influence my grandparents, Sill and Ibbie Weaver Rice, had on me and my life, but the more I reflect on my association with them, the more I think it was profound. Hardly a day goes by but that I don't think of them, one way or another, and it was Grandpa Rice who gave me a few mementos from his ancestors, suggesting that I ought to keep these relics and "start you a little museum of these old-timey things sometime."

My mother, Ruth Rice Irwin, is shown here serving a home-fixed snack to her father (Grandpa Rice) on his last trip to visit old Henry Rice's grave on Lost Creek in Union County. Henry, father of fourteen children, was 101 years old when he was buried there in the wilderness, and hundreds of his kin are now buried in that lonely graveyard. (Photo by John Rice Irwin, 1962).

My kind and gentle grandfather, Marcellus Moss Rice, at age 91. (Photo by Dan Hicks, 1963).

This picture was taken with my grandpa, Marcellus Moss
Rice, while I was home on furlough from the Army in 1951.
(Photo by my mother, Ruth Rice Irwin).

Chapter IV
College and the Army

After graduating from Norris High School in the spring of 1949, I spent the summer helping my father and brother David on the farm. I recently read the diary I had kept during this period and I was surprised at the relationship I had with my kinfolks on the farm. We "swapped" work with my Uncle Roger and Earl and Paul, and with my Uncle Morrell. We took Grandpa and Granny Irwin to church at least once or twice a week. We visited Grandpa and Granny Rice, and they often spent time helping us with the farm work. When the grandparents came to see us, the visitation was invariably combined with utilitarian activities—to help can beans, make kraut, or "put up" peaches, etc. In reading the diary for the first time in sixty years, I was reminded of the importance of church meetings—two or three times each week. It also reminded me of the frequent visitation among our kinfolk, before folks became distracted by modern-day disruptions such as television and cell phones.

Somewhere along the way I solidified my thinking to the extent that there was a better way to extend my learning and education than attending college and that my time would be better spent by self-discipline, reading, and perseverance. I was never convinced that sitting in a classroom day after day, year after year, listening to a lecturer would be meaningful to me.

But I gradually and reluctantly changed my mind and decided that I'd give college a try. One day in the summer of 1949 two of my high school classmates, Bobby Wallace and Jerry Lambdin, came by my house and announced that they were on their way to enroll in Tennessee Technological University, a state-run school located in Cookeville, some 120 miles to the west and about half-way between our place and Nashville. After a good bit of cajoling on their part I decided to join them—after all, it would be an adventure, I thought, and the little farm on which we lived, on a one-lane dusty road, held little promise for either adventure or romance.

So I packed a few essentials in a single, small cardboard grip and off we went, with my poor mother questioning my sudden and unplanned venture. I had a few dollars of my own money and it never occurred to me to ask either of my parents for money, although they would have readily given it. They were agreeable for me to go to college, I think, but they were not insistent. (When I returned home after a few weeks my brother David remembers that my Daddy asked me if I needed any money and I told him that I was getting by pretty well, but he gave me $65.00 nevertheless, and I'm sure he thought he was being liberal, not realizing the cost of room and board, tuition, books, etc.)

When we arrived in the pretty and historic town of Cookeville, home of Tennessee Technological University, located at the foothills of the Cumberland Plateau, we soon found that there were no dormitory rooms or other available rooms in the nearby residences—after all, this was only a day or two before classes were to begin. My two companions, Bobby and Jerry, had prearranged for their lodging and I spent the first two nights sleeping on the floor of their room.

Finally, just before dark on the third day after we arrived I found a vacant room near the old courthouse, a mile from the school itself. It was the epitome of Spartanism, with only the bed, two chairs, and a small closet. It was an upstairs room with no heat—only a tiny coal-burning fireplace and a coal pile in back of the house from which I could carry the fuel.

But I loved that old part of town and the friendly people with whom I soon became acquainted and I learned to improvise a routine which I found to be quite satisfactory. I would rise early and dress in the unheated room, not bothering to build a fire. I would then walk down Jefferson Street to the college. There were apple trees in several of the yards, and in the summer and late fall there was enough fruit alongside the streets of the old homes for my breakfast, different varieties from the various times of the season. I ate in the school cafeteria at noon, spending only 25 cents or so. When I wasn't attending class I would read and study in the library. I'd stay in the library or attend class until the library closed at 9:00 in the evening, and then walk to the town square where I could get a bowl of beef stew and crackers from a little restaurant for 25 cents; so my daily expenditure for food was about 50 cents. One night I was a little late getting to the café, and I noticed that the proprietor was placing lids and covers over all the food and I asked the purpose. He forthrightly told me that this was to keep the prevalent mice and rats away from the food.

Mrs. Drake, my landlord, was a kind lady and allowed me to sit in her living room on weekends and at night and read from her collection of classic history books, such as "The Rise and Fall of the Roman Empire", etc.

In my first semester I registered for a heavy load of courses, especially for a freshman. Additionally, I became an active member of the debate team under the renowned Professor Herman Pinkerton, whose debate teams won twelve state championships over his career. We met at night in his fine old home on Dixie Avenue, and we debated with other area schools. I also became circulation manager of the school paper, and I wrote feature stories for the town paper. In the late afternoon I worked as a gardener for the widow of a math professor, Dr. Hutchison.

On one occasion I told Mrs. Hutchison that as a debate team member, I had been invited to a banquet downtown and would need to finish my gardening early. After dressing for the occasion I rushed to my little café for my usual big bowl of beef stew, not knowing that the idea of a banquet was that food—supper—was to be served. I was surprised and embarrassed but didn't tell any of my friends of my bumble, and I managed to consume a second full evening meal. My education was extending beyond the classroom.

One professor, Dr. Lee, had a profound influence on my life. The course that she taught was Freshman English, which was a required course of all freshman enrollees, and as luck would have it, Dr. Lee, whom I had "drawn," had the reputation of being the toughest professor in the institution. It was commonly stated that one-third of her students dropped out of her classes within the first few weeks, another one-third failed the course, and the remaining third made only average, or below average, grades. Notwithstanding all these dire predictions, I'm convinced that I learned more under her tutelage than from any of my many other teachers.

Her method of teaching was not merely strict, but practicable and empirical. My former English teachers, even going back to junior high school, had stressed diagramming sentences, conjugation of verbs, and identification of the parts of speech—all the technical details regarding the language. Even if I had mastered the rote techniques, I'm not at all sure that there was any carry-over to the end product, i.e., improved speech and proper writing.

Dr. Lee taught by having her students write creative themes and mini-short stories. I was determined to dispel the dire warnings I had heard about her; and so I spent several hours writing my first theme, about Uncle Frank and his myriad antics.

When the corrected paper came back from Dr. Lee, she was most complimentary regarding my writing style and originality; but I received a big fat "F" on the paper. Any one mistake, such as a run-on sentence, or a sentence fragment, merited an automatic "F." On the next themes, I worked even harder and rewrote each one several times. Finally I received a "D," then "Cs," and eventually "As," and then even an "A+." Whatever success I've had in writing, I owe largely to Dr. Lee. I also learned from that experience that almost any negativism can be turned into something positive. The harder success comes, the more one appreciates it.

After three or four months rooming at Mrs. Drake's house I rented a room closer to the college and was joined by a roommate, Eugene Jared. He was raised on a small farm near the college and was as hard-working as I was and we often studied together, sometimes late at night; and on two or three occasions we literally studied throughout the night, going to early morning classes without even having gone to bed at all. He later became a successful (and I understand an outstanding) attorney there in Cookeville.

Our new landlords were Professor Ernest Lane and his wife. Their son-in-law, Jared Mattocks, was lieutenant governor of the State of Tennessee. He was also a respected lawyer and he hired me to carry a petition to the residences of Cookeville, a town of a few thousand people. The petition had something to do with the telephone company's plan to raise rates. Going from door-to-door was enjoyable and educational. I believe that I visited more homes in the town than any of its citizens.

During my freshman year at Tennessee Tech, I received frequent letters from my grandmothers, from Aunt Sophia, and especially often from my mother. Poor Granny Irwin, who was functionally illiterate, laboriously scribbled a letter to me every week or so. She said in one of her notes that she cried when she heard that I had I left for school. Every time I came home, I visited her and Grandpa, and she always had a "little present" for me, usually a fancy handkerchief, and she would slip "a dollar or two" into my pocket—hard and meager money she got from selling eggs.

There were several students from Anderson County at Tech and I soon made friends with several more students from various parts of Tennessee. I studied almost every day, but hitch-hiked throughout the area and I came home a time or two each month. Every time I came home, I would help milk the cows and assist in whatever farm work needed to be done—hauling hay, suckering tobacco, plowing corn, etc.

Although I was parsimonious while I was at Tech, I sometimes ran short of money. I note, from reviewing my diary, an example on one Thursday night when I was down to $1.00 and one lone Canadian penny. On the following day I purchased a 10-cent bag of peanuts and left on Friday and hitchhiked home, with 90 cents and the Canadian penny. I arrived home on Friday, in time to help with the milking and to partake of a great supper of my mother's making.

Although I had no means of transportation while at Tech I wanted to travel and visit the beautiful and richly historical Upper Cumberland area around Cookeville, part of which lay in what is commonly called the Cumberland Plateau. Although it was hilly and mostly unfit for cultivation and farming, and was especially isolated, that tiny area miraculously produced some of the most noteworthy persons of national stature.

Cordell Hull, for example, was born and reared a few miles from Cookeville. He was often called the second most influential and powerful figure in the country, perhaps in the world, in his day. He served as President Franklin D. Roosevelt's secretary of state during Roosevelt's presidency, from 1932 until FDR's death in 1945.

Mark Twain's parents lived in Jamestown, only an hour's drive away, and the world-famous Sgt. Alvin C. York, universally acclaimed as the greatest hero of World War I, was born and raised some forty-five miles from Cookeville, on the Wolfe River in the community of Pall Mall, Tennessee. Also, Abraham Lincoln's kinfolk lived a few miles to the north. (A few miles north of Cookeville, on the banks of the Cumberland River, there exists an old cemetery where, according to information from the Tennessee Historical Commission, one Abraham Lincoln, grandfather of "the" Abraham Lincoln, was killed by Indians.)

One Saturday morning I hitch-hiked to the ancestral home of Sam Davis where they were having a celebration in his honor. It was held at Davis' boyhood home, a palatial antebellum house in Smyrna, Tennessee, some sixty miles from Cookeville.

Sam Davis was called the "Boy Hero of the Confederacy." He was captured by Union officers during the war with incriminating papers on his person. Federal officials promised him his freedom if only he would divulge the name of the person from whom the confidential papers came. If he refused, he would be hanged. Young Sam refused to provide the source of the papers and he was hanged by the Union forces in the town of Pulaski, Tennessee, on Friday, November 27, 1863, at the age of twenty-one.

On one of my hitch-hiking forays, I visited a colony of Mennonites near Lawrenceburg on the Tennessee-Alabama state line. Although they clung to the horse and buggy way of life, they seemed to be most tolerant of other faiths, and they invited me to stay with them for two or three days. Their homes were without any decoration, pictures, or non-essential paraphernalia whatsoever. Their numbers were few and they were all kin, so there were no eligible, non-related individuals for the girls to marry. They were fine-looking girls, late teens and/or early twenties, and it finally occurred to me that the elders thought I may be a godsend for one of them, since I expressed a genuine interest in this religion. While I was staying there, the entire clan went to church—all except one handsome girl—but their ploy came to naught. I left the next day and hitch-hiked home.

During my stay at Tech I had my fiddle and guitar, and I tried mightily to learn the fiddle but without much success. I did a little better on the guitar. Although I thoroughly enjoyed my year at Tech, I decided to transfer to Lincoln Memorial University (L.M.U.), mainly because it was much closer to home.

I enrolled at L.M.U. for a quarter; then I entered the University of Tennessee School of Law. For several months, I had difficulty reading because of what the doctor described as eye strain. I rented an upstairs room near the Law School in Knoxville, and the prodigious amount of reading caused my eyes to become markedly worse. Finally I could hardly read at all. I had always had an inclination to become a lawyer, whetted during my years of debating.

Uncle Frank had always encouraged me to study law, and he was most pleased when I entered law school. But my eyes worsened, and I had no choice but to drop out. I got a ride to the Mountain Road, and I was walking home when I saw Uncle Frank sitting in his yard beneath his favorite shade tree. I had hoped that I would not see him and have to break the news to him, but I had no choice. He, as always, seemed most glad to see me; and the first question he asked was, "Well, how is school?" I could tell that he was most disappointed that I had dropped out, for he and I had talked extensively about my career.

Aunt Sophia said that tears came to his eyes when he broke the news to her—the first time that she ever saw him cry. A few weeks later he had a stroke, and I was with him when he died on November 1, 1951. Several neighbors came quietly to join the wake. I went out to his little wood shed by myself and wept uncontrollably.

I soon volunteered as a foot soldier in the U.S. Infantry during the earlier days of the Korean War. My ancestors had served in the military since the Revolutionary War, and they were proud of their military service. The Army seemed a patriotic and noble endeavor, promising as well to be adventurous and romantic.

I volunteered for the Army as an infantry private in 1950, during the Korean War, but served most of the two-year stint in Germany. I traveled pretty extensively through eleven European countries, studying the culture of my ancestors who had left there some 200-300 years previously.

I was soon thrust into the most rigorous infantry training at Fort Jackson, South Carolina. Day and night we sloshed through the rattlesnake-infested swamps and over sand dunes until I realized that these challenging and miserable conditions were anything BUT romantic, and void of anything remotely pleasant or adventurous.

The heat often rose to over 100 degrees Fahrenheit. Several soldiers suffered from heat stroke, and a few died as a result. We sometimes marched from 4:00 a.m. until midnight—twenty hours—with little water. Conditions became so severe that a Congressional investigation ensued and after a couple of congressmen visited us, conditions became somewhat less stressful.

From Fort Jackson, I was sent to Fort Benning, Georgia, for Officer's Training School (O.C.S.). Conditions here were even more challenging, almost unbelievable; I questioned even more the romantic and adventurous aspects of the military. Fort Benning was located on the Chattahoochee River, on the Georgia-Alabama line, and adjacent to Phoenix City, Alabama. Phoenix City was a "soldier town" and was notorious for its bars, saloons, and houses of ill repute. This somewhat lawless town was dubbed "Sin City, U.S.A." I went to the city once just to "check it out" and soon understood why it was the most "sinful" and lawless town in the country.

Soon after World War II ended in 1945, Russia sealed off her satellite countries from the rest of the world in what Winston Churchill called an "Iron Curtain." This canal was just one of the means used to enforce this barricade. Note that the ground alongside the canal is freshly dug; the guard(s) responsible for that area, it was commonly said, would be executed if such evidence were found of an escape. A young woman, I was told by local residents, was shot and killed at this spot while trying to escape the day before I took this photo. (Photo by John Rice Irwin).

Because of a back injury I was taken out of the Officers Training School and sent overseas. The captain of our outfit lined us up one day and read our orders, indicating whether we would be sent to Germany or Korea. As he neared my name of the roster, I, for the first time, became a little nervous and even scared. At the time American soldiers were being killed or wounded in the bleak and hostile mountains of Korea every day, and I remember thinking, "If he says Korea when my name is called, I may never again return to America." I had ambiguous feelings. On the one hand I longed for a combat zone, where I might help make a difference in protecting the poor South Korean people, and yet I had my life before me. If I had the choice of deciding my fate, I didn't know whether I would have chosen Korea or Germany, and I was glad that the choice was not mine to make. Finally my name was called. "Irwin, John Rice," the Captain bellowed out, and then he said, "Germany."

My mother Ruth, left, looking sad and worried as she and my dear Aunt Sophia say goodbye to me as I leave home for overseas duty.

After a few days at home I took a train to New York, where, after some two weeks, I took a troop ship to Bremerhaven, Germany. I was on the ship for over two weeks, and was deathly sick and heaving violently every single day. I would sit or lie on deck and let the cold mist sweep over and soak me, and my teeth would literally chatter incessantly. My bunk was down in the hull and we were packed in, four or five bunks high with no standing room. The stench from vomit was overpowering and the sounds of sick soldiers moaning and vomiting never stopped.

After some four or five days without any food, I went to the latrine and for the first time looked into the mirror. I could hardly believe what I saw. My face was totally white from the saltwater and I was gaunt beyond belief. I promised myself a hundred times that I would make every effort to gain a discharge and fly home from Europe when my tour of duty in Germany was over. I thought, too, of my ancestors who had spent many weeks and even months in conditions much worse than those I experienced here, and where death was a common, even daily, occurrence. I could understand why the vessels were often called "coffin ships." I thought, too, of the horror of the mothers who had to bury their babies and young children at sea. How terrible and how little we appreciate the tribulations our forefathers went through so their descendents could have a life of freedom and prosperity. How dare we complain of the miniscule adversities that we encounter.

After arrival in Germany, I was stationed in Aschaffenburg in northwest Bavaria, and while stationed there I bought an American car, a Chevrolet, which was a large car by German standards. I traveled extensively throughout eleven different countries on weekends, securing three-day passes and furloughs. I learned to understand and speak a little German, which was necessary in the rural and isolated areas, while most of the citizens in the cities spoke some English.

Just a few years after the Germans and Americans were killing one another in the war, the Americans were in Germany as occupation troops and the German youngsters followed us around in friendly admiration, as shown here in the next two photos. (Photo by John Rice Irwin).

I'm shown here, at right, with a fellow U.S. soldier in Germany with a German youth who, along with other local children, followed us on maneuvers.

Some of my ancestors were of German descent and I felt a kinship to the German people, although my ancestors had left the old country two or three hundred years earlier. I could see the resemblance between the rural German people and my people at home, which I thought remarkable. (Most of my ancestors, however, were Scots-Irish, English, and Welsh.)

World War II had ended only five or six years earlier and the bombed-out cities were a reminder of the destruction and devastation of the war. Germany's agriculture had been reduced by the war to the point that it was now carried out in its most primitive form. Many of the men and boys had been killed in those horrible years of warfare and much of the farming was carried on by the women. They depended, to a great extent, on cattle and oxen for plowing and cultivation of the fields, much as

farmers had done a thousand or more years earlier. (I visited the mainland of Europe a few years later and it was most remarkable that modern techniques had replaced these primitive methods.)

Some of the large cities remained almost totally destroyed when I was there in 1951. People were still living in the rubble and bombed-out buildings. In the large city of Cologne, for example, one could drive for miles and see nothing but the skeletal remains of once graceful edifices. One exception was the great Cologne Cathedral, the construction of which, I was informed, was started in the 1200s and finished more than 500 years later in the 1800s. It stood as a tribute to man's ingenuity and resolve, and it is a marvel to behold. I used to drive to Cologne every few weeks, and the spires of this great church would appear in the misty horizon miles before one could see any sign of the great City of Cologne itself.

But my personal goal was to learn as much as I could about the history and background of Germany and its several neighboring countries, and paramount and contemporary at this time was the Iron Curtain, a topic of world-wide interest and concern.

After the end of the greatest and most disastrous war the world had known up to that time, Germany was divided among the major victors: the United States, France, Great Britain, and the Soviet Union. The United States was bent on establishing a democratic government in their sphere: West Germany. The Soviets were intent, on the other hand, to establish domination over East Germany, under the absolute thumb of the Soviet Union. They sealed off East Germany and secured its borders in an absolute fashion and forbade ingress and egress across its borders. The border between East Germany and West Germany was so absolute that British Prime Minister Winston Churchill dubbed it the Iron Curtain, and it thereafter was referred to thusly. The Iron Curtain extended for an incredible 4,000 miles, a thousand miles longer than the distance from Maine to California.

Reading about the Iron Curtain was dramatic, but seeing it first-hand was even more revealing. My first chance was when my regiment (the 16th Infantry) was deployed in a training encampment in a former German compound in an isolated place at Grafenwoehr, near the Iron Curtain. One Sunday afternoon I decided to walk two or three miles in the forest and wilderness to the infamous barrier, just to see what the Iron Curtain looked like. When I arrived at the invisible "Wall," I first saw no sign of a demarcation, except a small sign printed in German, which read "Attention: Soviet Territory—Do Not Enter." But there was no evidence of any guards. There was, I was told later, a 200- to 300-foot-wide strip onto which neither American nor Soviet soldiers, nor civilians from either side, were allowed to enter. All was quiet there in the pristine wilderness and I decided to enter the "no man's land." I had only taken a few steps when two Russian soldiers popped up, fully armed and uniformed, and they bellowed out, with guns pointed toward me, "Achtung, Achtung!" I realized that the 4,250 miles of the Iron Curtain merited its name, and I quickly retreated.

"No man's land" on the "Iron Curtain" in Northern Germany near Lubeck.

A few months later, I spent four days in the home of my German girlfriend's family from which I visited the Iron Curtain near the town of Lubeck. We went out to look at the nearby "Curtain," which was on a small river or canal and on the Soviet side was the aforementioned "no man's land"—a frequently plowed area some 200 yards wide. Every few hundred yards there was a guard tower manned day and night by armed Soviet soldiers. Just the day before our visit a young German girl had tried to swim the river in darkness but was caught in the beam of one of the searchlights from the guard tower and was killed just before she reached the American zone. The cultivated area, I was told, was inspected frequently to detect footprints of would-be escapees and the tower guards were held responsible and harshly punished if footprints were detected.

On another occasion, on a bright sunny Sunday morning, at another location near the town of Lubeck, my German girlfriend and I again visited the "Curtain." There were several Germans standing along the "no man's land" area looking over to the Soviet side. I remember that there was a gaggle of geese on the American side and the Germans were amused and remarked, "Even the geese know better than to go onto 'no man's land'." I couldn't see any sign of military guards on the Soviet side and expressed doubt about the surveillance of Russian soldiers. In an endeavor to show my "bravery" before my girlfriend, I stepped into the "no man's land." Immediately there appeared from the bramble three armed Russian soldiers yelling, "Achtung, Achtung!" Of course I once again quickly retreated.

The cost of the manpower and the maintenance of the strict surveillance must have been extremely expensive and was totally ridiculous on the part of the Russians.

For a year I was stationed in the old medieval town of Aschaffenburg on the beautiful River Rhine. I was in charge of issuing supplies to the soldiers, and we often participated in large parades—to keep in shape, and, I suppose, to impress the German populace.

But I associated with the country folk in the little villages, and even spent some nights in houses which were clean and tidy, but which were shared with the farm animals, especially cows and oxen. I also toured some of the main edifices in the eleven European countries I visited—but I preferred the little back country villages where I would dine in rustic inns that were hundreds of years old.

Chapter V
Adventures in Writing, Real Estate, Collecting Mountain Relics, and Finishing My Education

After returning home from the Army in 1953, I bought a new car and re-enrolled in Lincoln Memorial University, in that bucolic and historic area where the states of Virginia, Kentucky, and Tennessee meet. I registered for a full load of classes and soon got a part-time job as a feature writer for the *Middlesboro (Kentucky) Daily News*. I became active in the Veterans Club at L.M.U. and was elected president of the organization.

I went back to my former landlady, Mrs. C. P. Williams, and I took four brown leghorn hens from home. We kept the hens in a pen in Mrs. Williams' backyard, and fed them on table scraps. We got three or four eggs each day, enough for our breakfast. (I lay claim to being the only student to ever take laying hens to college.) I planted a little garden in Mrs. Williams' backyard and it produced enough vegetables during the summer for our use. I would occasionally bring some bacon, potatoes, and other foodstuffs from home and Mrs. Williams made good use of the fruits of our little garden and the victuals mother sent from home. In return for my contributions, Mrs. Williams did the cooking and provided me with a rent-free room (my rent had previously been $10.00 per month). She was a great Southern cook, originally from a farm in Georgia, and she managed to stretch our scant food supply to the maximum.

Her house was in view of the famous Cumberland Gap, the gateway to the old West. The entire region was steeped in history, and I enjoyed exploring the back roads and writing about the people and places for the Middlesboro paper.

It was during this time that I met my future wife, Elizabeth Ann McDaniel. Her grandfather was a former sheriff of nearby Lee County, Virginia (as was her great-grandfather). Elizabeth's mother, Ethel Giles, was one of the seventeen children of Sheriff Giles, and her Grandfather McDaniel had been a dentist in nearby Tazewell, Tennessee. Elizabeth and I were soon thereafter married and

remained so for fifty-five years, until her untimely passing in 2009.

It was during this time period that I began to express an interest in acquiring the relics and chattels of the region, although I was preoccupied with school work and writing for the newspaper. But I sometimes slipped in a little time to ferret out some gems of that most pristine and beautiful region.

For example, Elizabeth and I had spent a Saturday night with her parents in Kingsport, Tennessee, and it was going to be a couple of hours before the noon meal. I thought I'd drive the few miles over into Virginia to "accomplish something." I took the old River Road at Clinchport, Virginia, and stopped at the first home place I came to. It was a small, relatively new brick house, not at all suggestive that it would have old-time pioneer relics. But I had learned that antique "pickers" tend to pass up such places and to go to old homes, and seldom were attracted to new houses such as this. I had learned, also, that many of the modern houses had replaced the old log homesteads and that the heirloom pieces had been moved to the newer houses, or relegated to the outbuilding, or to the basement. So I stopped there and found a gentle and friendly old gentleman who said that he didn't have any antiques. After a while of talking, I sort of steered him toward the open garage portion of the house and asked him if I could look inside and he readily agreed. I was able to buy several pioneer-era items, always with an eye on a beautiful piece of furniture in the corner of the garage. It was what is commonly referred to as a Jackson press, with wood and glass doors, and it was in pristine condition. It was filled with old tools and ordinary discards, and he was reluctant to sell the "press." "Where would I put all the plunder I have in it?" he asked. I told him that I'd pay him enough to buy two or three modern cabinets to store his relics in, and then he agreed to sell it.

I've bought a few thousand pieces of antique furniture, but this one rates among the top two or three pieces I've ever found. It was plain and simple in design, yet elegant in its simplicity and it was made entirely of native black walnut. The "press" was popular when President Andrew Jackson occupied the White House in the 1830s and 1840s; hence, I'm informed, the origin of the name "Jackson" press. We loaded it into my van and we were both happy with the trade. I paid him a fair price (I'm proud to say that the people from whom I bought items almost invariably said that I was a "high buyer" and they looked forward to seeing me).

I relate this little story as an example of how I acquired the bits and pieces of what would later become the Museum of Appalachia. I was back at my in-laws' house in time for a sumptuous late noonday meal, and I had made good use of the few hours of idle time.

I graduated magna cum laude from Lincoln Memorial University in 1954 and soon learned that I had been accepted for admission to Georgetown University in Washington, D.C. I had aspired for a career in the Foreign Service, and Georgetown was especially renowned as preparatory for such a career.

In the meantime, we learned that Elizabeth and I were expecting our first child and my financial status was not good, so I got a job as a teacher at Norris (Tennessee) High School until I could better afford Georgetown. At the same time, I received a stipend from the University of Tennessee to teach political science in the evenings.

My years teaching at Norris High School were most interesting and rewarding. But since I was the newest and the youngest member of the faculty, I was relegated to assume classes and extra-curricular assignments from which other teachers shied away. I was assigned to teach seven classes, in English, history, journalism, civics, etc., and I became the sponsor of the senior class and was put in charge of the school yearbook and the school paper, in addition to the daily preparations of seven classes. Twice each week I taught a three-hour evening class at the University of Tennessee in political science.

After two years as a teacher at Norris High School, I became principal of Melbourne, a small rural school in Anderson County. In addition to the principalship, I taught all of the subjects in both the seventh and eighth grades. I also became the lunchroom manager and coach of both the girls' and boys' basketball teams.

I had acquired my real estate license and worked in my spare time selling houses and small parcels of land. I also worked on and, in 1963, completed the hardback biography of my grandfather, *Marcellus Moss Rice and his Big Valley Kinsmen.*

At this time I had been elected as a justice of the peace, or squire, for the county. In addition to having certain judicial powers, the squires served as the main legislative body of the county. One of the many peripheral powers of a squire was that of writing warrants, marrying couples, etc. Quite frequently, I'd have to turn the class over to a responsible student and go down to the unfinished basement to marry a couple. I remember when a young would-be couple came by one day while I was teaching a class in Geography, wanting me to marry them. I hesitated to marry such a young couple until they brought their parents; then I agreed to conduct the ceremony. The prospective groom was to report to the Army later in the day.

I didn't have the "written ceremony" for the marriage; so I called Squire Everett Cox and his wife read me the short ceremony over the phone. I copied it onto one of those brown paper towels, and we were in business. In short order I had married the couple and I was back to my geography class within a few minutes.

The experience in this "poverty-stricken" mountain area stood in stark contrast to the graduate students (and even professors), which I would be teaching a few hours later at the University of Tennessee. I had little rest and long hours during this time, but I enjoyed the contrast in experience. My main regret is that I didn't spend more time with my wife Elizabeth and our two daughters, Karen and Elaine.

I soon became aware of the lack of hygiene among the students at Melbourne and that concerned me greatly, even more so than their educational needs. The year was 1959 and to my knowledge not a single student had ever been to a doctor, or certainly not to a dentist. Their teeth had decayed beyond redemption. In conjunction with the county health department, we started a program to correct the problem.

There was a pert little girl, for example, named Imogene, who learned quickly but who had no health care. She was in the sixth grade and I had received a report that she was smoking and using snuff. One day I asked her if she dipped snuff and smoked and she answered forthrightly, "Lord, God, Yeah. I've been smoking and dipping since I was in the first grade." I knew that she was one of seven children, living back at the foot of the mountain in a little two-room tenant house, and that her father, who reputedly had a drinking problem, only worked occasionally.

I asked a county nurse to come by to examine the students for dental deficiency and she found not a single student that didn't have decayed teeth—several of whom had teeth decayed down to the gums. What folly it is to think that we can interest children in verbs, nouns, or the Roman Empire when they are malnourished and suffering from health and/or dental problems.

These children were generally polite and appreciative of any assistance, and many became productive citizens. I later hired four of Imogene's brothers to work here at the Museum.

In 1960 I was assigned the principalship of Lake City Elementary School, the largest grade school in the county, and it was housed in a modern building. I was the youngest of the twenty-seven teachers in the facility, which presented a challenge for me.

I noticed that the modern cafeteria was devoid of any pictures or decorations—just blank concrete block walls, and the same was true of the long hallways. One of the first things I did was to post colorful pictures on these spaces. We started having interesting and entertaining weekly assembly programs in the auditorium, and I don't think the academic aspects of the school suffered, but improved as a result.

During the last few weeks of my first year as principal I learned that the Anderson County Commission had elected me as superintendent of the county schools. It was one of the state's largest county school systems, comprised of some 700 teachers, aides, maintenance workers, bus drivers, and other school personnel, as well as 20,000 students.

Suddenly, as superintendent, I found myself in charge of several hundred employees, and with no administrative training for such a position. My small administrative staff was professional, but untrained for such an endeavor.

During the seven years I held the position of superintendent, I was re-elected unanimously three times for the position, but resigned shortly after the start of my third term. During my tenure I worked with my staff to start several new programs: a county-wide Head Start program for pre-school-age students, and a neighborhood youth corps program whereby high school students would be paid for maintenance and grounds work.

Soon after I was elected superintendent, an event took place which might be called an important happening for the beginning of the Museum. My office was open five days of the week and until noon on Saturdays. One afternoon I heard of an auction sale to be held at the old Charles Miller homestead on the historic Clinch River. Being naturally curious and interested in such things, I attended the auction. As I drove down the dead-end river road, I came upon a plethora of ancient pioneer relics piled alongside the lane leading to the old home place. There were relics from the quaint old house and from a half-dozen auxiliary structures—the large barn, the smokehouse, corn crib, an old mill, the woodshed, the granary, and several other farm-related wooden buildings.

It was a warm spring day and the river flowed gently by the homestead and there was not another sign of civilization in sight. Apple blossoms and flowers graced the landscape around the old house, and one could hardly imagine a more peaceful and picturesque home place. This enhanced the appeal of the farm-related relics and household chattels, and I joined in with a few dozen men and women bidding on colorful quilts, old cane-bottomed chairs, pie safes, corner cupboards, and the like. I bought enough pieces to whet my interest, and this was the beginning of my fondness for collecting. One item, for example, was a wooden bucket which had been fished from the Clinch River during the great Barren Creek flood of 1916. This was the beginning of my inclination to keep notes and records of the histories and the backgrounds of the artifacts I acquired, tying the items to an event, an interesting or historic family, or person.

I also became interested in purchasing real estate. One of the most frequent questions I am asked by Museum visitors revolves around the source of my financial ability to acquire the real estate and the houses comprising the Museum, as if I were privy to unlimited amounts of wealth. The truth, of course, was that I had no money or wealth in the beginning. I often state, in response to queries of this sort, that I spent ninety-eight percent of my time and energies in collecting relics for the Museum, and only two percent of my time in buying and selling real estate; but that the inverse was true when it came to profits. I also started two small corporations and a few small businesses.

When I was a student at Lincoln Memorial University, I stopped by to visit one of my great uncles, S. T. Weaver, in Knoxville. He had a rather extensive factory and specialized in manufacturing flour- and corn-grinding equipment. During this infrequent visit with him, he offered to sell me a wooded tract which adjoined his father's place. It was a mile in length and several hundred feet wide.

I bought it, and, in order to save a surveyor's fee, I used a little hand-held compass to survey it and to arrive at the metes and bounds. I soon sold it for more than twice the amount I paid for it. All the profit from this and other transactions I put into what was to become the Museum of Appalachia.

I bought a beautiful farm near the Museum and divided it into smaller ten- to fifteen-acre tracts. I personally laid out the road, without the help of a surveyor, taking into consideration the creek and the groves of trees. With the help of a single worker, I laid out and installed the water line and the streets. I drew the "division map" and readily sold the parcels of the beautiful old farm based on a map which was hand-drawn on a piece of poster paper. The parcels sold for an aggregate of three times the purchase price. Again, all of this profit went into the development of the Museum.

I read somewhere that the great entrepreneur Cecil Rhodes once said that no transaction was a good one unless both parties were satisfied and pleased with the deal. I have given this simple admonishment a lot of thought over the years, and I've come to the conclusion that this is a great truism.

I have made ninety-eight additional real estate transactions in my spare time, and one day I decided that I needed to decide which road I wanted to travel: to concentrate on real estate, or to put my time and energies into the development of the fledgling Museum.

I had an old friend who had become quite wealthy in the coal and timber development business, and especially in buying and selling real estate properties. He owned thousands of acres of timber, farm, and coal land, and he owned a prosperous bank, a country club, and numerous other real estate and business holdings. I reasoned that even if I put all my time and energies into expanding my real estate endeavors, I would likely never approach his wealth, and even if I did, I would not have contributed very much to society, and to my people—not as I could by showcasing my great friends, and the wonderful people of Appalachia, by developing the Museum. So, simply put, I decided on building and developing the Museum of Appalachia as a tribute and lasting memorial to those great and unsung folk of the Southern Appalachian Mountains, rather than just making money.

I should note here that I developed an unofficial partnership with Cathy Brown, a friend of the family, a real estate agent, and the first woman mayor of Clinton, Tennessee. Her knowledge of real estate and her common-sense approach to trading was phenomenal. We never had any kind of written contract, but we trusted one another totally, and we both purported that our word would always be as good as our bond and it consistently worked out that way.

Cathy came to me one day to ask about selling a tract of land I owned. She said that she could get $60,000 more than I was asking for it if I'd agree to sell it in small tracts. She knew that I had promised the adjacent property owners that I would not sell it in small lots, and I told her that, even though there was no written contract with the neighboring property owners, I would honor my word even though it meant a great financial loss. She said she knew what my answer would be, but she felt obliged to ask me nevertheless.

Although I stopped pursuing my real estate endeavors, I did occasionally buy and sell farm land and houses when I encountered them. All the profits from these undertakings I put into acquiring artifacts (and real estate) toward developing the Museum, which became my consuming passion.

Chapter VI
School Superintendent
(1962 - 1969)
and Director of the Tennessee Appalachia
Education Cooperative
(1969 - 1982)

John Rice Irwin at his desk soon after he was appointed superintendent of the Anderson County, Tennessee, school system, c. 1963.

The eight years I served as Anderson County superintendent of schools were among the most challenging and difficult of my career. As noted previously, in 1962 the Anderson County Commission unanimously elected me as the Superintendent of the county school system, whereupon I was the youngest superintendent of the 150 school systems in the state. I thought also that I was doubtless one of the most ill-prepared for such a task. I was virtually without training or experience for such a position.

I nonetheless accomplished four major achievements during my tenure. First, I consolidated several small isolated mountain schools with larger and better-equipped schools, and I remodeled and improved other schools in the district. The consolidations were almost always met with opposition from the local communities. For example, there was one small school which qualified for only two teachers. First, it was difficult to hire qualified teachers to serve under such demanding conditions, and secondly, the student transportation and other costs were far in excess of that of larger schools. But the tiny schoolhouse of Laurel Grove had once been the center of community activities and the battle cry of those opposed to the closing of the school was that it was "centrally located."

I did agree to meet with the community leaders one afternoon to discuss the advantages their children would receive in a nearby and larger school. The feelings ran exceedingly high in the little community on the appointed day of the meeting, and someone had sprinkled the school's driveway with roofing nails in the area where I usually parked. I used a different parking area on the day of the meeting, and half of those attending got flat tires from the ruse, while I escaped unscathed. This had the effect of further infuriating some of the community leaders.

In other cases where we closed smaller schools, community leaders contacted the Knoxville television stations and newspapers and advised them of angry gatherings in opposition to local school closings. Such closings were touted as taking the heart out of the respective communities, and nightly television coverage followed the events. Numerous threats were made against me and the school board members but we stood firm in our resolve and in our position that the students would be much better served in larger facilities. After the consolidation, I believe that all agreed it was for the better.

Anderson County served a most diverse population, including part of Oak Ridge (widely reputed to have more per capita PhDs than any city in the country) as well as the extreme rural and isolated mountain communities. Some of the more adamant opponents to consolidation were bent on having their way, through hook or crook, or through brute force. On three separate occasions, men carrying guns ferreted me out and demanded that I concede to their strongly held positions. I finally agreed to meet with one citizen early Sunday morning at the nearby Little Senator restaurant, which I owned and operated. He showed the pistol he was carrying and announced that he was not leaving until I agreed to back down in my support of closing the local school. I told him that I would never back down from my position, and if he felt that strongly, he had the weapon and I had none, and for him to do what he had to do. He, of course, left and I heard no more from him.

Other highlights of my superintendency were of more importance and were more civil in nature. We started one of the first county-wide Head Start (kindergarten) programs in the state, which proved to be one of the most beneficial early education programs, especially for the rural and isolated areas of the county. We had one of the first Neighborhood Youth Corps programs where students could work and be paid for projects on school and/or public properties.

I worked with my board and the county commission to build a large, state-of-the-art high school in Clinton. It received national note for its innovative features and was chosen for display as a model school building at the National School Administrators' Convention, held in Atlantic City, New Jersey. (Much of the credit for the design and building of this facility goes to the architect, John

Soon after I became superintendent of the Anderson County School System in the early 1960s, we built this modern school building, which was used as a model for other schools in various parts of the country. (Photo courtesy of Anderson County School's website).

Shaver of Celina, Kansas; and to members of the school board.)

During the last two or three years of my tenure as superintendent I joined with the seven other superintendents of the adjoining school systems to promote an innovative and revolutionary idea regarding educational administration: the educational cooperative, known formally as the Tennessee Appalachia Education Cooperative. This idea held out more hope of a wider scope than any such new concept with which I had been associated. The idea is as simple as it is revolutionary. Basically, it involves the concept that many programs can be much more efficiently and effectively conducted when several systems pool their resources and conduct a program, or programs, as a common project. One example is that of Heavy Equipment Mechanics and Operational Training. No one system could muster enough funds for the highly expensive pieces of equipment the course would require. But together they could acquire the machines, enabling students from the various school systems to reap the benefits of the training.

Together, we acquired used machinery, most notably from TVA and other governmental agencies, which we repaired and refurbished in a training setting; and we completed much-needed projects such as drainage and retaining walls and recreation areas which served both for training and practical purposes.

There was, however, one major problem. The individual school systems could not claim these improvements as their own. They had to share all positive accomplishments and outcomes with the "educational cooperative." When we received praise for projects in the individual school system, then it went to the cooperative and not to the individual school superintendent and/or the respective school boards. Despite these inherent problems over who would receive credit for any improvements and programs, the cooperative was able to accomplish a great deal.

I became active not only in the local cooperatives but also in the National Consortium of School Cooperatives, which was gaining some national recognition. In 1982 I was elected president of the National Cooperative Association.

Driver's education, which no single school system could afford, was another program the cooperative started. We devised a system which eliminated the "one teacher, one student" approach. We set up radio contact whereby one teacher could coordinate a dozen or more students in a large parking lot; and this one teacher could direct students in practicing parallel parking, angle parking, starting and stopping, etc. The teacher could monitor and have direct contact with each student. This system received national attention.

After the cooperative had employed a number of other innovative ideas, the seven superintendents saw the need for a single individual to head up and direct the program; whereupon they asked me to become director of this organization. I resigned as superintendent of Anderson County Schools in 1969,

and accepted the title of executive director of the Tennessee Appalachia Education Cooperative—a position I held from 1969 until 1982.

During this time, I worked under the direction of the seven superintendents of the respective school systems that comprised my board of directors. We initiated several new programs, which I administered with a small but efficient staff. After a while, we were organized to the extent that I felt that the organization did not need my full-time services. Although the funding for these programs, and for my salary, was from federal grants, I surmised that my job did not merit a full-time salary. Without consulting my board, I informed them that I was reducing my salary, and my involvement with the cooperative, by fifty percent. The Board informed me that it was satisfied with my performance and that it was not necessary to reduce my salary, but I did so nevertheless. I felt that I should not get a full-time salary when only half-time work was required for successful performance of the position.

Within a few months I reported to the board that my staff could run the various programs without my involvement, and I resigned the position as executive director and gave up an attractive salary. This was in 1982, and I started, for the first time, to devote my full attention to the expansion and development of the Museum and to related projects.

Chapter VII
The Museum Of Appalachia And How It Came To Be

I have alluded in passing to the numerous business and trading ventures over the years that provided the capital upon which I founded and developed the Museum of Appalachia. These ventures began when I was quite young.

When I was fourteen years old I became partners with my Uncle Frank for raising a patch of tobacco on his farm. He had a small "allotment" from the government, but he was unable to tend it. We agreed that I could have the half-acre allotment and the land to grow it on and I'd plant and attend it and prepare it for market for half of the proceeds. I cultivated the plot with a four-foot plow and one of our old mules.

Another of my early "ventures" was when I bought and resold a few 'possum and muskrat hides for a profit of 10 to 15 cents per hide. My first real "business," I think, was when I was twelve or thirteen years old, when I partnered with the venerable Elmer Sherwood in trapping. I furnished the traps and Elmer furnished the "know-how" and we divided equally skunk, muskrat, 'possum, and an occasional mink hide.

Later, when David and I were in our mid-teens, we returned to the chicken-raising business in a big way. We raised some 100 chickens at a time and peddled them in Clinton when they reached fryer size.

I became a "restaurateur" in 1955 when I built and opened a restaurant, The Little Senator, named after Senator George Norris, the "Father" of the Tennessee Valley Authority, just outside Norris, Tennessee. As my wife, Elizabeth, and I were on our way to see her mother one Friday afternoon, I noticed a small hand-painted "For Sale" sign in the weeds on a lot near our home. I told her that it looked like a good location for a "drive-in" restaurant, and that if it were still for sale when we returned I would buy it and build a drive-in.

So, when we returned Sunday, late in the afternoon, I found the owner and bought the lot. This small restaurant, being the only one of its kind in the area, became a most popular gathering place for adults as well as for teenagers and it was almost always crowded.

Later, I bought a boundary of timber from my Uncle Morrell. I hired my old friends, Ed and Elmer Sherwood, to cut the logs and I engaged John Eckerly to haul them to the saw mill. We cut and hauled some 60,000 board feet of logs and I made a few thousand dollars on the enterprise.

It was about this time that I opened a small fruit and produce market in the lot behind the Little Senator Restaurant. I didn't have the time to oversee it and it was only moderately successful. Within a few months I bought a large dirt-floored shed in Clinton and opened up another fruit, vegetable, and produce market, buying produce from the farmers' market in Knoxville.

One of the first pieces of property I purchased was from my Uncle Roger. I sold half of it to my brother and I then sold four large lots to the Sherwood brothers. They were some of the hardest working and most honest men I have ever known. They developed their "little farms" from the small tracts they had bought from me and they were in their glory with their own land. They had worked all their lives for landlords, but had never acquired any land of their own.

There was an old farm house on this property and it was considered worthless by everyone who viewed it. "Tear it down and get it off the property," they would say. The porch was rotted off, but with a small amount of used lumber I replaced the porch and painted it. There were small pieces of siding which I replaced, also with used lumber. I painted the entire house, painted the roof green, and replaced several windows. It became an attractive old house at a cost of less than $1,000.00 for the repairs.

I sold the house to a hard-working old fox hunter, Ike Anderson, who had never been able to acquire a piece of land. There was enough open land with the house to pasture his cow and raise a garden big

Brothers Roy and Ed Sherwood are shown here plowing with Old Maud, the Museum's donkey. The Sherwood brothers helped to develop the Museum from its earliest day. (Photo by Pulitzer Prize Winner Robin Hood).

enough to pretty much sustain his family. He paid me $15.00 per week on the house, and was most elated to have a place of his own. He was never a day late on his payment. Ike would bring me his $15.00 every Saturday morning, usually so early that we were still in bed.

I more than doubled my original investment in the land, but my greatest reward was the satisfaction resulting from helping these gracious men in their waning years in getting a piece of land of their own. They worked prodigiously in improving the premises and in raising large, productive vegetable gardens.

When I started teaching in Norris High School I purchased a partially finished modern three-bedroom house between Clinton and Oak Ridge and completed it, along with the landscaping; and after a year I traded it for a beautiful five-acre tract near Norris. I used stone which I dug from the yard and from my father's farm and built a beautiful stone house, where I reside to this day.

There was a farm adjoining our property of approximately 100 acres of grown-up and neglected land, known as the "old Keith place," which later became the nucleus of the Museum of Appalachia. One day Jake Butcher called me about selling me the old Keith place; this turned out to be one of the most important telephone calls I ever received. Jake and his brother, C. H. Butcher, had emerged from their isolated Union County farm and had expanded, almost overnight, into the real estate and banking businesses. They soon acquired several farms and businesses, and they bought several banks, including the large Knoxville-based Hamilton Bank.

I told Jake that the acreage pretty much surrounded my little piece of land and my greatest desire would be to have a bit of the land, but that I had little money. "How much of it do you want?" he asked. "Well, it would be great to get five acres," I told him. I later became more reckless and told him that I'd like to have nine acres, and then I became even more reckless and asked about the entire 100 acres, but again, I had little money.

"If you want the entire farm," he retorted, "you can have it for just what we're paying for it. Don't worry about the money—-we'll work that out." A few days later, I was astonished to get a copy of the deed from him, with no down payment required. "You're one of Dad's favorite friends, and he'd want us to satisfy you," Jake told me.

So, I had the deed, free and unencumbered, and that area now embraces the extended Museum of Appalachia, and several adjacent tracts. I sold a few parcels off this large farm, enough to pay for the entire farm, with some eighty acres left over. So, through the trust and generosity of the Butcher family, I acquired enough land for the Museum with several acres left.

One day I was in a lawyer's office in Clinton and my sometimes partner Cathy Brown was there and she asked me if I'd be interested in partnering with her in buying a large tract of land. She showed me a map of the property, which was near Roane State Community College. I said "yes," and agreed to go into partnership with her. I had not been on the property, but I could see no way we could lose money on the venture. It consisted of several hundred acres, and was over five miles in circumference. No surveying, no soil tests, no checking on zoning regulations, etc. I eventually sold my share to Cathy, for a "reasonable" profit.

The most interesting property I purchased was an historic old mansion in Knoxville once owned by the relatives of the playwright Tennessee Williams, and it was also the ancestral home of the founder of Knoxville. I sold the property for a reasonable profit.

Perhaps the most profitable piece of land I bought was a farm just across the road from the Museum. After I bought it on the open market I went over to the beautiful place with a piece of poster board and I spent several hours sketching how best to divide the property in large (five- to twenty-five-acre) tracts. I drew in where a road could be built for access—no planner, no surveyor, no engineer. I took into consideration the serpentine Buffalo Creek, which wends its way through the property, and the grove of beautiful mature red cedar trees in "laying out" the road and the lots. I then set a price for each tract, including the acreage where the large white farmhouse stood, and when I added up the prices of the aggregate of these tracts that I

assessed, it totaled almost exactly three times what I paid for the large tract. Within less than two years, I had sold it for my asking price, netting nearly a quarter of a million dollars in profit. Again I put all the profit into the Museum.

During this period, I purchased a four-story corn and wheat mill on Little River near the foot of the Great Smoky Mountains in Blount County. I soon partnered with four local businessmen, all friends, and formed a corporation of which I became president. The mill was fully operational and we ground meal and flour and distributed it throughout the greater community—mainly to country stores and small markets. The mill produced stone-ground products and was powered by the waters from the river. It was pretty heavily mechanized and required much upkeep, and we didn't have the time or the expertise to set up a distribution system to compete with the large competitors, so we sold this beautiful complex after some two years.

At one time I owned property in six East Tennessee counties and in the cities of Knoxville, Clinton, and Norris. After several years of working with real estate, I considered whether I should concentrate on dealing in real estate where I felt that I could do well monetarily, or whether I should put my time and energies toward "making a difference" in helping people through the preservation of the history of our people and our culture.

I decided not to deal in real estate, but to concentrate on the Museum and in preserving the heritage of the great and noble people of the Southern Appalachian Mountains, and that is what I did. I continued to buy real estate when I "ran across" it, but I didn't actively pursue real estate interests. My thoughts, energies, and resources were forever after directed toward the Museum and its growth and development.

I entered the world of authorship when I wrote the book "Alex Stewart, Portrait of a Pioneer" in 1985, which proved to be one of my greatest challenges, and eventually the most successful of my endeavors. It was published by Schiffer Publishing in Pennsylvania, distributed nationally, and remains in print after twenty-five years. I've received more "love" letters on this work than on the Museum of Appalachia itself. I eventually wrote and published nine additional books, eight of which remain in print and are distributed nationally; some of them are distributed to several foreign countries. (I mentioned earlier that I had written a hardback biography of my Grandfather Rice in 1963.)

This highway entrance sign on State Highway 61 designates the "turn-off" onto the lane leading to the Museum of Appalachia. (Photo by Jim Marziotti).

The main entrance for visitors to the Museum of Appalachia.
(Photo by Nell Moore).

Chapter VIII
Serious Years of Collecting for the Museum
(1970-1982)

Almost without exception, those who tour the Museum of Appalachia ask about its origins—who put it together, how the collections were acquired, what inspired and motivated the originator to embark on this mission, and especially how it was financed.

The germ of the Museum, though I was not at the time aware of it, goes back to when I was a small tyke spending time with my grandparents, my parents, and other kith and kin. For example, I remember with great fondness spending time with Granny Irwin on cold winter days in her cozy and aromatic kitchen; I recall, with equal nostalgia, playing in the cedar shavings and watching Grandpa Rice making ax handles and apple boxes. These images, and a thousand more, lay latent for decades; they manifested themselves when I started collecting and repairing mementos reflective of those bucolic times.

First, I should perhaps say that, in my early years of collecting, I had not the vaguest notion of starting a museum. I acquired items belonging to my extended family and from old friends as a way of remembering those cherished kindred. I relied on buying the items, and never asked for donations. I felt much more comfortable with this approach.

Grandpa Rice would occasionally give David and me an old wooden plane or a worn-out drawing knife which had belonged to old George Rice, or to Uncle Jim Rice the gun maker, admonishing us that we should save these heirloom pieces and start us a little museum sometime. Likewise, Granny Irwin would give us a flax hatchet or a walking cane which belonged to her grandfather, with similar admonishments.

We devoted a small space for these few items in the corner of our upstairs bedroom. I added a piece now and then. The first item I recall acquiring was the old hand-cranked coffee grinder from my Uncle Frank when I was thirteen or fourteen years old.

It was several years later that I became serious about collecting. There was an old wagon maker by the name of Nen Gaylor who plied his trade in nearby Dutch Valley, and after his death one of his daughters asked if I would be interested in purchasing some of his tools. I was amazed that he had so many early artifacts and relics, and I bought a truckload of these pieces, some of which dated back to the pre-Civil War era. I had bought several items from the old Miller auction, previously mentioned, and the garage was filled, so I had to pile these items outside in the weather, and I borrowed a tarpaulin from my father to cover them.

The door to the log spring house and granary was locked, but I had developed a good eye for sizing up the contents of a building by merely peeping in through the cracks. My travelling companion, Wallace Denny, took this candid shot as I peered into this building on the old Daw Buckner homestead in Penhook, in nearby Union County, Tennessee. (Photo by Wallace Denny, October 1974)

I stopped by Foust Hollow Road to visit with two neighbors, Fiddlin' Bob Cox, at left, and Ike Bumgartner, who were clearing off a hillside for a spring potato patch. (Photo by Gary Hamilton, 1980)

Rowe Martin, who lived near the birthplace of the renowned Davy Crockett, was a bachelor and a pack rat of the first order. One could maneuver through his large house only by following narrow trails. He also had barns and sheds equally piled to the brim. I bought hundreds of interesting, historic, and unusual pieces from him over the years. He is shown here conjuring up a trade with me on his back porch. (Photo by Elizabeth Irwin, October 1979)

John Rice, at right, is shown here with Johnny Harness at Johnny's log home in Laurel Grove with his wife in the background. Chris Phillips, a noted writer, is pictured in the center. (Photo by Frank Hoffman)

This whetted my appetite and these early additions fed my enthusiasm. I started traveling the mountains and back roads literally going from house to house. It was not easy to do. There is a certain approach one must use—here stands a total stranger dressed in a coat and tie, asking about buying antiques, and though I knew the ways of the people, the first inquiry was most often not a successful one. I remember one time I spent three days in Southwest Virginia, upper East Tennessee, and Western North Carolina buying only two or three insignificant items. In order to save time and money, I slept in a motel for $2.00 a night, or stayed with a friend.

At this juncture I'll give an example of one of my most successful ventures. An old gentleman and neighbor, W. G. Lenoir, commonly referred to as General Lenoir, became one of my closest friends. He and I traveled the hinterlands and back roads for almost a half century. He was collecting for his museum, now the state-run W. G. Lenoir Museum in Norris Dam State Park. We never had any problems in dividing up the items we had bought on a particular trip.

One day he told me of an old-fashioned blacksmith and machine shop in the historic town of Loudon on the Tennessee River. He said that he had spent decades trying to purchase the relics from the long-closed shop and that he was giving me all the information he had relative to this treasure trove. He had given up on ever buying it and he said that he hoped that I would have better luck than he had.

W.G. (General) Lenoir accompanied me on thousands of trips in the mountains collecting relics from the past. He is shown here retrieving a home-made tricycle from the old Sharp place near Norma, Tennessee. (Photo by John Rice Irwin, ca. 1980)

The owner of this large blacksmith and early machine shop, Don Galbreath, was a cordial and friendly old gentleman but he was not willing to even talk of selling any of the contents of the shop. It had belonged to his deceased wife's family, and had been a fixture there in Loudon for generations. Although he left no hope of ever parting with it, I kept in touch. First, I wrote him a letter, thanking him for talking with me. I enclosed a good bit of information and photographs on the Museum. When I was in the area of Loudon, I'd stop and talk briefly with him and we became pretty good friends, but not close enough that he would price anything to me. I learned that there was a large collection of the family's personal and historical items stored in the upstairs portion of the shop area, and that some were from the Governor Taylor family. Brothers Robert and Alf Taylor had both been governors of Tennessee and they were legendary in Tennessee history. They often campaigned together, and Bob was an old-time fiddler which helped garner the large crowds which they drew when they campaigned and debated one another.

After a few years, and after my persistent but gentle prodding of Don Galbreath with regard to my acquiring his collection had produced no result, I wrote him another letter, thanking him for being so patient with me and informing him that I was still most interested in purchasing the items, but that I would not pursue the matter any further. But I told him that if, sometime in the future, he decided to sell, then I would appreciate the chance to discuss the matter with him.

Weeks passed, then months, then years, and I did not hear from him. But, after fifteen long years, I received a hand-scrawled note from Don informing me that he had "about" decided to sell the contents of the estate, and for me to come by. He had dozens, maybe even hundreds, of people wanting to "get in and look at all the stuff," he said, but he had refused all inquiries because he said he wanted to give me first chance.

Keep in mind that I had never even seen the family, household, and personal items stored upstairs. When I did go there with Don, I was more than amazed at the extent and the quality of the historical collection.

After we reached an agreement on a price for purchasing the estate, I had my Museum employees bring three of my old trucks down and we loaded them until dark. The next morning we were back to load more of these historic relics, and even then there were more loads to be removed. I can say in all honesty that there were more quality items in

this group than I've seen in some small museums. It contained, for example, the best extraordinary quilts, dozens of unusual crocks and jugs, numbers of ornate picture frames, writing desks, and almost every kind of household item one can imagine. It even contained, neatly pressed and packed away, KKK hoods and robes. (There was a time when the Klan was less disrespected and disgraced than it later became, and prominent citizens sometimes joined. Hugo Black, who later became one of the respected Supreme Court justices, was a Klansman in his younger days, as was the revered Senator Robert Byrd of West Virginia.)

I describe the acquisition of the Don Galbreath collection for two reasons: First, it illustrates the need for, and the results of, perseverance; and secondly, it illustrates the importance of being honest and forthright with people. I came to genuinely like Don Galbreath and I knew that he liked me in return. I wasn't "buttering him up" for the sake of ulterior purposes, and he was very much cognizant of this fact.

I'll relate here a similar experience where these attributes worked to my advantage and to the benefit of the Museum. I had heard of the old Rufus Elledge homestead in an isolated community called Rainbow at the foot of the Great Smoky Mountains in Sevier County. I had heard that the family was living in a true pioneer setting and in pioneer conditions. I had also heard that they lived in a log house surrounded by a dozen log and other frontier-style outbuildings, all of which were filled with early chattels; but I was also told that they would not part with any of their ancestral possessions, and that they detested anyone even trying to buy them.

But nevertheless one morning I drove to this most isolated and picturesque homeplace, at the end of a narrow dirt road, and I found a resolute little woman on the porch, stringing and breaking beans. I, as always, was dressed in my superintendent's regalia of black coat and tie, and I drove an impressive Chrysler (I never believed, as some "pickers" did,

In going through the recesses of Tommy Cline's woodshed in a hollow in Monroe County, Tennessee, in the 1970s, we found this old groundhog hide banjo which he had made for himself many years earlier. He readily agreed to sell it to me, and it is now on display in the Hall of Fame at the Museum. (Photo by John Rice Irwin)

I bought many rare mountain items from Tyler Bunch of Snake Hollow, a true mountain man if there ever was one. His wife keeps busy with her quilting in the background while Tyler and I traded. (Photo by Pulitzer Prize recipient Robin Hood, c. 1985)

that I should try to fool the people by wearing overalls and a flannel shirt). Her name, I was to learn, was Kellie Elledge; I learned that she was born and raised on this homeplace. I introduced myself and told her that I was starting a little Museum north of Knoxville and that I was buying old antique items with which to furnish the log houses on display there. "We have these people from Gatlinburg and Pigeon Forge drive up here all the time," Kellie informed me, "and they got to be a bother."

"We're not selling anything to anybody," Kellie continued. In an endeavor to emphasize her resolve, Kellie emptied the bean strings from her apron and lifted it, revealing a little .38 caliber pistol in a front pocket of her dress. "Do you know why I keep this pistol with me?" she asked. And before I could answer she said, "I carry this gun with me for antique people who come around here, trying to

buy our old stuff. We ain't got nothing to sell!", and I believed her.

About this time her husband, Rufus Elledge, came in from his forage in the back fields carrying a large bundle of six-foot-long hog weeds. He was a large and imposing man and he reminded me of the great Sgt. Alvin C. York. Rufus seemed impressed that I would know that the weeds were for his hogs. After "proper" introduction I said, "Rufus, we had a neighbor that didn't have any corn and he fattened two hogs on nothing but hog weeds and a little slop. Did you ever hear of that?" "Yes, sir," he responded, somewhat enthusiastically, "I've done that myself."

Rufus also carried a Kentucky rifle and a fox horn, and before long we were "old friends" talking about fox hunting, muzzle loading rifles, etc. Then I said, "Rufus, Kellie said she carried that pistol under her apron for antique buyers. Do you think she'd shoot me for trying to buy these old relics?" "Well," Rufus responded in a friendly manner, "her bark is worse than her bite, but she shore don' want to part with any of these old family relics."

I did not pursue the matter further, so I just took a few pictures and sat down and helped Kellie break some beans, and then I was on my way. Soon after I returned home I sent several enlarged pictures which I had taken of them and the next time I was in the vicinity I found a most friendly Kellie and Rufus Elledge. I don't know whether or not they even had photos of themselves at the time, but they seemed most pleased to have the ones I had sent.

Kellie and Rufus were sitting beneath a little covered walkway between the kitchen of their house and the smoke house, peeling and quartering apples. They were remarkably friendly this time and invited me to "have a seat." After discussing which old-time apples were best for drying, and how long it took to dry them in the sun, I asked them if I could peer into the nearby smokehouse, and they readily agreed. There was a hand-made "soap barrel" bound with split hickory saplings near the door. It was filled with cakes of year-old home-made soap, and they seemed surprised that I would be interested in it, and they were even more surprised when I offered them $20.00 for it. They pointed out that the soap had "dried out" and was not usable. I realized then that their definition of an antique was quite different from my definition. I bought some molasses barrels and other items, but I didn't press my luck by trying to buy too much.

The next time I visited the Elledges, Kellie invited me to go through the loom house and "pile out" anything that I was interested in. She had several spinster aunts, she told me, who had spent much of their days in the big loom house making great coverlets, hand-spun rugs, etc., plying their trade and packing these colorful and beautiful textiles into long chests. She and Rufus readily agreed to part with these beautiful and unusual woven materials. I left with my van filled to the brim. Kellie was a totally transformed lady from the pistol-packing woman I had first met. We were now fast friends.

It was several months later before I traversed the area again, and I drove up to the old Elledge

Old-time mountain music is played daily at the Museum, where visitors often join in traditional and familiar songs. Shown here in this winter scene playing around the open fire are local musicians, left to right, Herb Miller, Fiddling Charley Acuff, and Jim Russell.

homeplace. But things were now different. There was no sign of life, and an aura of abandonment had settled over the place. There lay on the front porch, for example, a beautiful corner cupboard and other "discards." It was obvious that the former occupants no longer lived there. I drove down to the main road and soon found the home of one of their sons, and as luck would have it, the place where Rufus was then living. "You've been on my mind a lot," Rufus greeted me by saying. "You know that Kellie died, and I moved in with my son here. There's a lot of 'plunder' up there on the old home place and I wanted you to have first chance for anything you wanted."

This was before the advent of the cell phone. I asked his son if I could use his telephone and he readily agreed. I called John Eckerly, who worked for me at the Museum periodically. "John," I said, "I'm up here in Sevier County in the Smoky Mountains and I need for you to bring your big cattle truck here and get a load of antiques." He said, "Shoot, it's spitting snow up here and it's supposed to get worse." I said, "John, this is very important—I need for you to put your high cattle gates on the truck. I'll pay all your expenses and I'll even pay for your truck if you wreck it, but I need you to get up here."

"I think it's a dumb thing going up in them mountains with all the snow they're predicting, but I'll start out," John answered grumpily. I gave him the directions and he was phenomenal in following them.

John arrived in late morning and it was snowing and he was still complaining about the folly of getting out in such bad weather. All day long Rufus and I went from one old building to another, loading items from the pioneer period onto the truck.

At dusk on this blustery day, the snowflakes continued to fly, but with little accumulation; and finally there was not space for another single item in the high truck bed. I kept notes on each item I purchased—and altogether, there were enough items to start a small antique museum.

From the beginnings of my collecting, I was more interested in the history and background of a piece than its intrinsic value—who made, used, repaired, and passed the item down to the sons and daughters. For example, "old" Uncle Campbell Sharp, when it was too wet to plow, would spend the day wandering over his pastures cutting the hateful thistles. A cow would steer clear of these prickly, spiny plants, and hence deprive the bovine creatures of the grass that grew around them. Uncle Campbell had an oft repaired old iron hoe that had been made by his pioneer ancestor, old stationmaster Bill Sharp,

from iron made from a local furnace. He called it, almost lovingly, his "thistle hoe."

I attended the public auction many years later, when they sold Uncle Campbell's possessions, and in the rush and din of auctioning off a pile of old tools and broken items, I saw that one lot of miscellaneous items included that "four-Sharp generation" thistle hoe, worn down to the nub, and worthless monetarily. I bought the entire lot of miscellaneous items for $4.00. Today, Uncle Campbell's thistle hoe hangs on the porch of the General Bunch House at the Museum, a standing reminder of the five generations who had a hand in making, repairing, and using it down through the years.

I kept copious notes regarding the history and background of most of the tens of thousands of other items I have bought over the years. I think this practice has had much to do with the love and acceptance expressed by the visitors to the Museum.

It took me a long time to appreciate how much items displayed in the Museum mean to those people who are connected with the items, either by relation or by association. We have tens of thousands of school-age students visit the Museum each year, and whenever a student from Harlan County, Kentucky, or Morgan County, Tennessee, sees a piece which belonged to his or her relative, they are elated, drawing the attention of their school mates.

For example, I bought numerous items from an old timer, Sam Brown. Sam was a true Appalachian man if I ever knew one. I met him in 1960, when he was sixty-five years old. For several years hence he has helped me to tear down and remove log cabins in the Hancock County area to the Museum of Appalachia. He had the reputation of being one of the hardest working men in the county and I never doubted that assertion.

He lived in a poor rocky valley in the community of Treadway, and he worked as a day laborer for anyone who needed help. He would walk for miles to work, and arrive at daybreak, for a twelve-hour work day. He was a pack rat of the first order, and his house and outbuildings were filled to the brim.

Some fifty years later his daughter, Susan Brown Vaughn, called and asked me if she could visit the Museum to see some of the items I had purchased from her father. She did visit the Museum and brought a dozen of Sam's kin, and after the visit I received the following letter from Sam's granddaughter. When people ask me why I spend all my time, effort, and money, I could not do worse in responding to the question than to let them read this letter:

The Peters Homestead House, with the Loom House nearby, is a focal point from the Museum's meadow.

Dear Mr. Irwin:

We recently visited the Museum we had a great time it is amazing, beautiful, and truly wonderful place everyone had a good time and felt deeply blessed to have been there especially together has a family to have shared a day in such a peaceful place. Thank you so very much for making that dream come true for each of us we are truly greatful so Thank you from the depths of our hearts. Thank you so much from each and everyone of us. This was even closer to our hearts because we are the Sam Brown Family his granddaughter cried when she saw his picture and said it's as if Papaw is right here with us also his great-grandson was leaving in a few days after we where thereto go away to the Army and his grandmother (Sam's daughter Susan Brown Vaughn) promised him this vacation trip before he left, so that was our last family vacation with our Army boy for a while. Thank you again and again.

THE SAM BROWN FAMILY
Susan Brown Vaughn (Sam's Daughter)
Leonard Vaughn (Susan's Husband)
Davey Dale Seals (Sam's Grandson)
Kay Seals (Davey Dale's Wife)
Donna Seals (Sam's Granddaughter)
Joshua Seals (Davey Dale's Son and Sam's Great Grandson)
Chastity Seals (Joshua's wife)
Latasha Seals (Davy Dale's Daughter and Sam's Great Granddaughter)
Dakota Seals (Donna's Son and Sam's Great Grandson)—Our Army Boy
Kordell Burton (Donna's Son, Sam's Great Grandson)
Blake Seals (Joshua's Son, Sam's Great-Great Grandson)

We hope to come back again real soon. Thank you very much.
The Sam Brown Family, All 11 of us.
May God Bless you and your family greatly.

Sam Brown lived in a little unpainted house on Mountain Valley Road of Hancock County, Tennessee, which was once considered to be the second poorest county in the United States. But Sam, like his neighbors, managed to support his family in that narrow, rocky valley. Any time I had a house or barn to be dismantled, I got Sam to help. He was a dynamo at taking down, loading, and moving old buildings, and I always thought he could do the work of two ordinary men. (Photo by Frank Hoffman, November 1977, at Sam's home)

This "perpetual motion machine" was designed and handmade by Asa Jackson, a farmer from near Lebanon, Tennessee, prior to the Civil War. It's opined by scholars to be one of only two known to exist in the world. This one, on display at the Museum, has been studied extensively as to why and how it was designed to run forever without any source of power. Even the great scientist Sir Isaac Newton tried unsuccessfully to perfect such a device.

My emphasis on small, human-interest items should not override the fact that there are numerous, one-of-a-kind historic items in the Museum. For example, there is a large "perpetual motion" machine reputed to be one of only two known to exist in the world. It is made of some 200 hand-carved wooden precision parts, and ideally would run "forever" without any power. Many attempts have been made to develop such a device through the ages, including efforts by the English genius and scientist, Sir Isaac Newton, but none were successful. The one in the Museum was made over several decades by an ingenious man, Asa Jackson, who lived near the town of Lebanon in Middle Tennessee. When the Civil War loomed on the horizon, Asa feared that the marauders would destroy his handiwork of half a century, or that, at the least, they would steal the secret of his invention. In an endeavor to protect his invention, he hid it in a large cave near Murfreesboro, Tennessee, until the war was over.

Apparently Asa was not able to market his perpetual motion machine and it ended up in an old barn belonging to his grandson. There it rested until it was re-discovered in 1990 by a friend of mine, Dr. Charles Wolfe. While researching the music of Jack Jackson, grandson of Asa, Dr. Wolfe saw this odd configuration in multiple pieces. Dr. Wolfe alerted me of his discovery, and I immediately contacted the Jackson family and was able to purchase it. I restored it pretty much to its original form.

The Associated Press ran a story on the "machine" and subsequent interest resulted. For example, there were four notable physicists from Oak Ridge who visited the Museum on four separate occasions to study the perpetual motion machine. I don't think that it ran perpetually for them, but they were intrigued with the matrix of precision parts and they were most especially interested in "how" it was supposed to work. These internationally renowned physicists employed the help of their compatriots in this respect, but I never learned of their final thoughts on the subject.

Someone entered the "machine" on the internet after I had displayed it at the Museum—and one person, David W. R. Brown, responded enthusiastically. He had spent years studying perpetual motion contrivances and he surmised that there were only two such "complete" machines— this one and another in Germany. He spent months dissecting this one here at the Museum and he wrote a book detailing the intricacies of the Asa Jackson machine. The book, with hundreds of diagrams, is entitled *The Asa Jackson Perpetual Motion Wheel*; it is available at the Museum.

In the same vein as the perpetual motion machine, there is displayed here a combination cotton and ginning machine, which scholars say pre-dates Eli Whitney's patented machine. Mr. Brown claims that there are only three or four known to exist.

This team of oxen, Jacob and Esau, is being driven by Jim Stafford at the Museum. These twins weighed approximately 1,000 pounds each. Oxen were the most common draft animals in early frontier times.

The interior and exterior of the historic Arnwine Cabin, which is considered by many to be the smallest in the country to be included in the National Register of Historic Places. (Photos by Nell Moore)

There are tens of thousands of interesting, unusual, and, I think, historically important items on display in the numerous cabins at the Museum and it is most difficult to convey to the reader the extent of this collection. We get numerous notes and letters from people who have toured. Many of their comments are so flattering and complimentary that I'm reluctant, and even embarrassed, to mention them, but I'll do so nevertheless. There are two basic types: first are comments from individuals who have visited and toured the museum, and secondly are comments from the national press.

Like many people, I acquired a few items from friends and kinsfolk as a means of remembering them, and for no other purpose. I went a little further than most, and my small garage became filled, and then overflowing. At first I piled the artifacts outside and I continued to collect, and that's when it occurred to me that it would be good to acquire a log cabin to store the antique articles. This was the extent of my ambition. But after acquiring the General Bunch house, I continued to collect, and before long this cabin was also filled, then I bought another, and another. Over the years, I acquired and moved some seventy more buildings; I also built several large two, three, and four-story display structures. Again, this did not fulfill my ambitions.

It was then that a few local people started dropping by to investigate. Sometimes, for example, when we returned from church we found two or three families loitering in and around the log cabins,

which were located, literally, in our backyard. It was then that I decided to add another cabin and open the little "complex" to the public, and charge an admission of 50 cents per person. We also catered to groups of school children.

I installed a service station-type hose which ran from the little parking lot to our dwelling, so that the bell would alert us that we had a visitor. Either my wife Elizabeth or one of our young daughters, Karen or Elaine, would take it "time about" in going out and greeting the visitors.

Even though we had precious few visitors, the occasional visitors became disruptive. So we decided to hire a part-time attendant, much to the delight of Elizabeth and our daughters.

The Irwin's Chapel log church was moved to the Museum from Madison County, North Carolina. It is used for weddings and singings on a regular basis. John Rice Irwin is shown standing in the doorway of the church.

The Hall of Fame contains hundreds of thousands of artifacts, purchased from the interesting and colorful people of the southern Appalachian region. Personal notes relate the stories of these items and of the people who used, cared for, and mended them. (Photo by Dick Doub)

This most simplistic beginning may be compared to some sixty buildings today, including four large display buildings, among them the Hall of Fame Building. The attendance has increased from a dozen or so per week to a few thousand, from throughout the country and from numerous foreign countries. The continued publicity in the form of films, magazines, and newspapers was paramount in this respect.

At one of the Museum's Homecomings, sisters Grace Rutherford and Alverta Stooksbury wash clothes in an open kettle, as was the custom in this area until the mid-1900s. (Photo by Dick Doub)

Thelma Phillips spins flax and cotton into thread while minding the corn bread and soup beans cooking over the open fireplace in the Homestead House at the Museum.

Dollie Haskins Turnbill of Hoskins Hollow was one of the great mountain women from whom I bought several coal mining and Appalachian artifacts. (Photo by John Rice Irwin)

Granny Cox Williams, standing, and her winter's catch of fur are shown here in this rare and interesting photograph. She lived near the Museum and trapped mainly on John's and Buffalo creeks, and is responsible for catching and skinning these varmints, including possum and skunks. The two youngsters pictured may be her grandchildren.

Chapter IX

What Old-Time Mountain Music Has
Meant to Me and to the Museum of Appalachia

My great uncle, Lee Irwin, was the celebrity in our family, not so much because he was a handsome gentleman farmer and cattleman, but because he was considered to be the greatest fiddler in the area. He had won contests throughout East Tennessee, Georgia, and in surrounding states. His style was not that of modern country music or even bluegrass. He played such pieces as "Bonaparte's Retreat," the "Merry Widow Waltz," "Over the Waves," and "Under the Double Eagle." His daughter, Lois, sometimes accompanied him on the piano. Even as a child I was enthralled with his playing. I had no way of knowing how great his influence would be on me.

When I served in the Army several years later,

in Germany, I bought a mandolin from a fellow soldier, Bill Ramsey, and learned to play. Soon after I returned from my tour of duty, we had a visitor from California. He was setting up a bus tour to this area, and he asked if we could provide food for a tour group, and if we could provide some old-time music. I told him that we could do both, and he scheduled his group to visit us. After he left, my wife Elizabeth said, "Why did you promise to feed and entertain this group? We don't have a band or the wherewithal to feed seventy-five people." I said, "We don't have a band or the means to cook for a group of this size now, but when they come we will be able to accommodate them."

In the early days of the development of the Museum, before we had formal stages, we used this farm wagon for performing. The Museum band members, from left, are Carlock Stooksbury, Carl Bean, Happy Jack Rogers, John Rice Irwin, Ted Wyrick, and Fiddling Bob Cox.

So, I got some of the local musicians together, we pulled out a hay wagon for a stage, and I employed a few local ladies to help prepare supper. The event was successful beyond our expectations. This group came back every year for the next twenty-four years, and they helped spread the word to other tour groups.

By the time the World's Fair came to Knoxville in 1982, we had the "Evening in Old Appalachia" show almost every night and sometimes 150 or more visitors would attend. The evening consisted of my band, a country meal, and a self-guided tour.

Wallace Denny, left, and my father, Glen Irwin, await the opening of one of the music shows at the 1982 Museum Homecoming.

My little band of four local neighbors playing from a hay wagon inspired the Tennessee Fall Homecoming, an event now featuring five stages and some 400 musicians. Homecoming annually draws visitors from all 50 states and from some 55 foreign countries. Through the years, these visitors have included many nationally known celebrities.

I'll try to summarize the remarkable growth of what came to be known as the Museum of Appalachia's Annual Tennessee Fall Homecoming. First, I need to admit that I did not have the vision or the foresight that the pitifully small gathering would gain the success which it did, and I'm indebted to a multitude of "helpers." But the story unfolds as follows.

As school superintendent in the 1960s, I always thought that our textbooks pretty much neglected any reference to the area now referred to as the Southern Appalachian region. The history books and other literature were largely published "up East" and there was scant literature on our region for our teachers to utilize.

One day in 1980, George Brosi, a friend of mine, asked me if he could bring his little trailer with a few books and printed materials related to our Southern Mountains and "set up" at the Museum on a certain weekend. I told him that I'd be most happy for him to do so and that I would charge him no commission, but that we only had two or three dozen visitors over a weekend, and that our parking lot would only accommodate 26 vehicles. George was not deterred by the dismal prospect that he would sell only a handful of his regional books.

I began to feel sorry for George and I decided to try and attract more visitors. There was a popular early morning television program in Knoxville, airing live from 6:00 to 7:00 a.m. when many working people were readying themselves for the work day. The folks there agreed to let me bring some old-time musicians and craftsmen for two or three days each week prior to the George's weekend event. I got my old mountain friends, Ed and Elmer Sherwood, to agree to go with me; I also took the great old-time fiddler Charlie Acuff and my friend Carl Bean, along with Byrd Brannon, and we had a studio full of the "genuine articles."

On the morning of the event, the 36 parking spaces were filled by 8:30 and cars were parked in the Museum fields and along both sides of the road. As more and more lines of traffic formed, I made arrangements with a neighbor to use his large contiguous pasture for parking. The music served to create an ambiance for the mule-powered cane mill and for the other old-time activities. That night, nearly 16 hours after the activities had started, I wrote in my journal, ". . .the people rolled in, first by the hundreds, and then by the thousands—never heard so many nice comments about an event such as this." The following day, there were even more visitors. And I was somewhat taken aback when the craftspeople and the visitors asked if we planned a similar event the next year; and for the first time I began to consider replicating the event.

Every old-time demonstrator, musician, and other participant returned when the event was scheduled the next year, in 1981. This reminded me of the traditional family homecomings I had attended during my childhood. Hence, the next such gathering, held in the spring of 1982, I called a "Homecoming." After that, since the event has been held only in the fall, it is called the "Annual Museum of Appalachia Tennessee Fall Homecoming."

A casual and passing incident comes to mind from one of the early Homecomings. I was walking toward the site of the molasses stir-off when I met a kindly old mountain man whom I'd known all my life. He'd

Dr. Nat Winston plays the bagpipes and often served as Master of Ceremonies at Homecomings. (Photo by Frank Hoffman, 1986)

been helping to shuck and shell corn and to operate the old corn mill. I mentioned that we appreciated his help and that I hoped he had enjoyed the weekend. He put his hands on my shoulders and looked me squarely in the eye. I noticed that he had trouble speaking. In a moment, he did speak—in a quivering voice. Literally with tears in his eyes, he said, "John Rice, I've lived a long time in these mountains, and I've had a lot of good times, but I've never enjoyed myself like I have these last two days—I never have. This has been the most enjoyable time in my life. I hope you have these Homecomings for as long as I live, and that I can come back every year. And then I hope you'll keep on having them for my children and my grandchildren." Then he turned and walked off into the fading October twilight, and into a slow, cool wind; and I knew then that I'd probably never stop having the Tennessee Fall Homecoming—not, anyway, 'til I get as old as my old friend. Maybe even then it will be continued.

The Museum is designed for visitors of all ages. Robert Spicer shows off some of his wee dancers on the main stage during Homecoming. (Photo by Frank Hoffman)

Harold Garrison from the mountains of Western North Carolina is shown here flirting with sisters Alverta Stooksbury and Grace Rutherford, interfering with the washing and rinsing of clothes. (Photo by Robin Hood)

My cousin, Carlock Stooksbury, plays the mouth bow for my wife, Elizabeth, and our youngest grandson, seven-month-old Will Meyer. Carlock was the most popular member of my old-time music band for some forty years. (Photo by John Rice Irwin, Summer 1991)

When the Museum first opened, groups and local musicians would spend Sunday afternoons making music here. From the left are Fiddlin' Bob Cox and Carlock Stooksbury playing the Jew's harp, as my father, Glen Irwin, on the right, listens hypnotically. (Photo by John Rice Irwin)

Archie Campbell, of national note as a radio and television entertainer and as a co-founder of the popular "Hee-Haw" TV series, is taught to quilt by the jovial lady, Opal Hatmaker, of the mountain community of Laurel Grove. One of thirteen children and without a father, she was five years of age when she learned the art of quilting from her mother. (Photo taken at the Museum Quilt Show by JRI, 1983)

The "Homecoming" eventually drew national attention. Alex Haley, the most popular writer in the country at the time, for example, embraced the event, and came every year from 1982 until his death in 1992. He enticed Brooke Shields, Oprah Winfrey, the actor Lavar Burton, five-time Grammy winner Quincy Jones, and a host of others to attend.

Alex Haley and John Rice Irwin

Dolly Parton is shown here with her mentor, Cas Walker, one of East Tennessee's most colorful and prosperous businessmen. Through his many radio and television shows, he is credited with starting the careers of 257 entertainers such as Tennessee Ernie Ford, the Everly Brothers, and, of course, Dolly Parton, whom he put on an early morning country music show to promote his supermarket chain. Dolly today gives Cas full credit for starting her career. The connection to the Museum is that Cas and I became rather close friends and he promoted the Museum, and especially the annual Homecoming, extensively on his many shows. He was a regular attendee to Homecoming himself, drawing thousands of people who "just wanted to see and meet him." (Photo by John Rice Irwin)

The entertainers' list reads literally like a "who's who" among old-time and bluegrass musicians: Earl Scruggs, the best known banjo player in the world; Bill Monroe, the "undisputed" father of Bluegrass music; the great Mac Wiseman; John Hartford; Dr. Ralph Stanley; and hundreds of others.

At one time we asked the audience to register their names and addresses indicating their respective home locations. In 45 minutes, people from 48 states had signed up, and before the day was over individuals from the two remaining states, Hawaii and Idaho, had also registered. Each year we have more than 50 persons from foreign countries register at the Homecoming.

The Tennessee Fall Homecoming was listed 17 times by the Southeast Tourism Society as one of 20 outstanding autumn events in the Southeast. The American Tour Bus Association listed Homecoming as one of its "TOP 100 EVENTS AND FESTIVALS" in the country.

After the World's Fair ended in 1982, I kept my little band together and we developed a package program which we called "An Evening in Old Appalachia." We served a supper in our auditorium, usually barbeque; then I would emcee and play with the band. I included a bit of local history and then the group toured the Museum complex. Some of the groups were local, but mostly they were from various parts of the country, and some from Europe and the Far East.

We also started traveling and playing for groups throughout East Tennessee, and always had audience participation—square dancing and such. In addition to appearing on the local TV stations, we played on several cable channels, such as the History Channel.

The inimitable Grandpa Jones never failed to draw thousands when he performed at the Museum's Tennessee Fall Homecoming.

The famous mandolin player, Red Rector, is shown here (center) playing informally at
one of the Tennessee Fall Homecomings at the Museum.

Carlock Stooksbury demonstrates the playing of the
mouth bow to the legendary Bill Monroe, "The Father
of Bluegrass Music" here at the Museum.

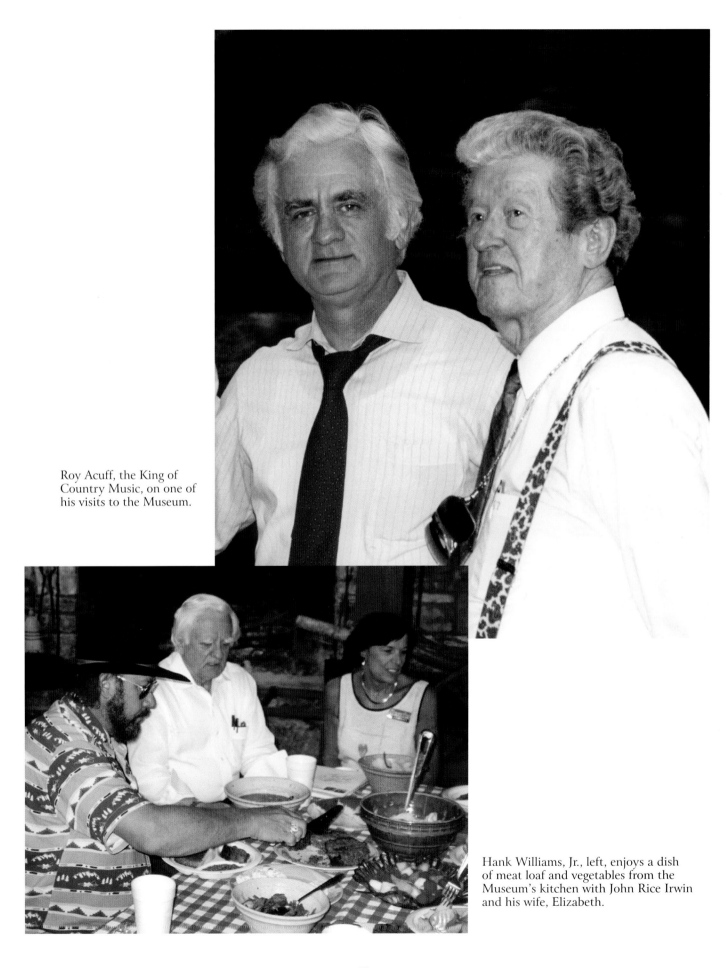

Roy Acuff, the King of Country Music, on one of his visits to the Museum.

Hank Williams, Jr., left, enjoys a dish of meat loaf and vegetables from the Museum's kitchen with John Rice Irwin and his wife, Elizabeth.

One of our most interesting shows was when we played for the Disney folks in Anaheim, California. The Disney people spent a good bit of time (several days) at the Museum; then they flew my entire band to the Disney Studios for final filming. They "featured" us daily in the big theater in the round for more than 20 years, and some of the local folks who happened to see us out there were duly impressed. Alex Haley persuaded several of the band members to go with him to Disney World in Orlando, Florida, to see the same film. It was, we thought, quite impressive to see ourselves on the giant screen, played throughout each day. I understand that the video of the band was also shown daily by the Disney folks in Japan and in Paris, France. We played what we called old-time mountain music, and we've been honored to play for such people as Brooke Shields; Oprah Winfrey; Hank Williams, Jr.; Quincy Jones; Mary Costa; Alex Haley; and numerous governors and U.S. senators. Folks from the Oak Ridge scientific community hosted some of the world's most prestigious scientists at their facility, and they almost always brought them here to get a taste of the region's culture.

The Museum of Appalachia Band members recording music at a Disney studio sound stage in California. They were featured in the famous "Studio in the Round," continuously played for some fifteen years in Disneyland in California and later daily in Disney World in Orlando, Florida, and then in Japan and Paris. Pictured are, front row, left to right: John Rice Irwin, Elizabeth Irwin, and David Ezell; second row, left to right: Joy King, Ray Rutherford, Charlie Acuff, Ron English, and Carlock Stooksbury. (Photo by Disney Studio)

My band is shown here at Disneyland Studios in California, recording for the large "Studio in the Round" which played our group's music for years, maybe decades. In the front left is David Ezell with the guitar and my wife, Elizabeth, playing spoons. On the back row, from left to right, are Joy King, Ray Rutherford playing bass, John Rice Irwin on the mandolin, Fiddlin' Charlie Acuff, Ron English, also playing fiddle, and Carlock Stooksbury playing the mouth bow. (Photo by Walt Disney Photographers)

Located on the Tennessee-Virginia State line, this log cabin, which spawned the famous Carter family music group is often credited as being the place where the most important early old-time music in America started. Country music icon A. P. Carter was raised here. I wrote a book, *The Story Behind the Story of Country Music*, and virtually every single person whom I interviewed gave credit to the Carter Family for their inspiration. I attended the largest old-time music festival in Northern Ireland and when I walked in I was brought to tears when I heard the popular Carter Family song, "Keep on the Sunny Side of Life." Joe Carter, the son of old A.P. and Sarah, was also born and raised in this log house. I acquired numerous items from the old Carter Family home. (Photo by John Rice Irwin, June 1991)

So, my early involvement with old-time music paid off over the years. All the members of the band were better musicians than I was, but maybe my emceeing made up for my musical deficiencies.

Sisters Aunt Polly Ann Arnwine and Aunt Jane Arnwine lived their entire lives in the tiny but historic Arnwine Cabin, which I moved to the Museum after it was abandoned. It is now listed on the National Registry of Historic Places.

Chapter X

The World's Fair and its Effect on the Museum

For several years certain Knoxville leaders and businessmen had been working on plans for Knoxville, Tennessee, to host the 1982 World's Fair. These efforts started in the late 1970s, when various metropolitan centers from throughout the world were likewise vying for the honor. Knoxville, which is located within a 20-minute drive from the Museum, had a population of some 150,000 people and was competing with cities of several million people. Few people took Knoxville's bid seriously. The name "Scruffy Little City" was even applied by some news networks when they were describing Knoxville.

In 1982, the World's Fair came to Knoxville and the "world" came to participate. The Museum of Appalachia, just eighteen miles away, helped to provide the entertainment. This photo shows the 266-foot high Sunsphere in the midst of the World's Fair site.

One individual who was dead serious about pursuing the prospect of having the World's Fair in Knoxville was a local farm boy from adjoining Union County, Jake Butcher. Jake and his family were longtime friends of my family, and Jake had left his small farm, with a single truck, and had gone into the oil and gasoline distribution business. He and his brother, C. H. Butcher, soon bought a small, local bank and soon thereafter acquired several farms and several other banks. Their rise in the business world was truly meteoric, and a few people began to take him seriously. As noted earlier, Jake bought an old farm adjoining my few acres, and eventually sold it to me for just what he paid for it—and fully financed it for me, as I had little money. This property later became the Museum of Appalachia.

First, I knew, or thought I knew, that the proposed Fair would bring thousands of tour buses. So I managed to get a list of more than 3,100 bus companies from throughout the country and I wrote each one a "somewhat personal" letter, extolling the virtues of the Museum, along with photographs and the national publicity we had received. Keep in mind that this was more than a year before the Fair was to open, and I was realistic enough that I did not expect much response—but I did expect some. Weeks passed, and then months, and then a year went by and still I had not heard from a single tour bus company. Some six months before the Fair was to open, I wrote a similar letter to the same tour bus companies, and again no response.

About three or four months before the much touted World's Fair was to open, I received a telephone call from a young lady in New York City who indicated that she represented Cosmos Tours of New York and London, and that she was coming to Knoxville and would like to meet with me. I knew that Cosmos was one of the premier tour companies in the country and in Europe, and of course I was anxious to meet with her. After touring the Museum she was sold on the idea of bringing all of her World's Fair tours here to experience the Museum, complete with Appalachian music by my band and a country supper. They planned to bring two or three tours here each week for what I had dubbed "An Evening in Old Appalachia." This, for us, was phenomenal.

When word got around that Cosmos had chosen us for a side trip for their tours to the Fair, other bus companies started making reservations to come here as well. Many were to bring their tours here on a regular basis throughout the six months' Fair for the full Evening in Old Appalachia program.

An important by-product of the many thousands of visitors we had during the World's Fair was that many of these folks planned to, and did, tell their friends and neighbors about the Museum, resulting in a prolonged and positive effect. Additionally, numerous magazine and newspaper articles throughout the country wrote articles featuring the Museum. There were several television documentaries and TV programs which resulted from the media exposure.

The direct and indirect benefits of the World's Fair to the Museum were no less than phenomenal, the effects of which continued years after the event ended. In addition to the tour buses, countless family groups visited the Museum during the Fair. Certainly one of the most important effects the Fair had on the Museum resulted in our involvement in recruiting the musical groups to participate in the Fair on a daily basis. The line-up of musical groups, as it turned out, included my Museum of Appalachia's old-time music band.

It happened thusly: The officers from the Fair wanted one segment of the Fair to include old time indigenous music and crafts, and they solicited my assistance. They called it the "World's Fair Folk Life Center."

So I held a well-advertised try-out program for participants to be held at the Museum, and hundreds of aspiring musicians and artisans came. I had three knowledgeable judges for the musicians, and the try-outs lasted for three days. We selected several outstanding acts which the World's Fair folks accepted. The "Museum of Appalachia Band" was promoted by the press as having been selected to be a part of the World's Fair, and this provided much favorable publicity for our band and for the Museum. Had it not been for the $4.00 guitar that I bought as a teenager from my cousin, Amos Stooksbury, and my subsequent interest in old-time string music, none of this, in all probability, would have happened.

This photograph illustrates the variety of people who visited the Museum. From the left is Levi Collins, a local mountain man, miller, and moonshiner; John Palmer, a nationally popular NBC anchor; Vitaly Korotich, the editor of *Ogonyok Magazine*, one of the most prominent Russian publications; and my cousin Horney Rogers, who, like Levi Collins, was a farmer, corn miller, and best known as a moonshiner of fine corn liquor. (Photo by Frank Hoffman, ca. 1985)

There were, of course, many exciting and outstanding exhibits from countries throughout the world. But by the admission of many observers, our own Folk Life Center was one of the most popular exhibits in the Fair. I played with my band in most of the band's performances and served as the emcee. I, of course, promoted the Museum liberally and frequently.

The Museum of Appalachia Band is shown here during one of their performances at the World's Fair in Knoxville in 1982. Standing, from left, are band members Hoot Osborne (on knee), Carlock Stooksbury, Joy King, John Rice Irwin, Elizabeth Irwin, Ray Rutherford, David Ezell, and Ron English. Seated in front are dancers Charlie and Cher McDonald and their daughter, Heidi.

Chapter XI

Some People Who Have Strongly Influenced Me and the Museum

It has been said that one's life is a composite of the personalities of people he has known, and I have found this to be true. This is especially true as it applies to the building and development of the Museum of Appalachia. Some of these people have contributed directly to the founding and the building of the Museum, while others have contributed indirectly. Some are nationally known and others are barely known outside their local environs. I'm listing a few of them here, in alphabetical order. I've divided these contributions into two parts: Celebrities of Fame and Notability, on the one hand, and Interesting and Colorful People on the other.

Celebrities of Fame and Notability

Senator Lamar Alexander

I'm not listing Lamar first because he has served eight years as Tennessee's governor, or because he served as the president of the University of Tennessee, or because he was the United States secretary of education, or because he was a viable candidate for president of the United States, or because he is one of the country's most powerful and respected U.S. senators.

I'm including him here because he comes first in the alphabet; because he is one of my closest friends and advisors; and because he became the first chairman of my Museum of Appalachia Board of Directors. He became a friend long before I was in any position to assist him in any kind of political way. He and his vivacious wife, Honey, and their family became friends and frequent visitors with our family, while their daughter, Katherine, worked with us one summer here at the Museum. When the Museum was officially transferred to a non-profit entity, Lamar

The writer Alex Haley, left; Tennessee Governor Lamar Alexander; and John Rice Irwin pause during a tour of the Museum during the Tennessee Fall Homecoming, c. 1988. (Photo by Robin Hood)

became chairman of the Board; and he resigned only after he was elected to the U. S. Senate, so that there would be no conflict of interest issue.

Lamar and I spent many days driving through the countryside, relaxing and buying relics and log cabins and log barns for the Alexander complex at the foot of the Great Smoky Mountains National Park. He is one of the most thoughtful, empathetic, and accommodating persons I have ever known. He has a genuine interest in the people he serves as senator, and he has been a genuine inspiration to me. He has stood by me in some troubling times, when fair-weather friends have shied away. He really believes in the Museum and what it stands for, and he has manifested this sentiment consistently. (After he became U. S. senator, he was instrumental in helping the Museum obtain a large federal grant.)

Minnie Pearl, the ever-popular Grand Ole Opry star, and Tennessee's Lamar Alexander with John Rice Irwin in the Irwin Chapel Church at the Museum.

Senator Howard H. Baker, Jr.

Howard H. Baker, Jr., is considered by many, including this writer, to be the most respected and admired elder statesman in the country. He and his wife Nancy are dear friends of the Museum and of the Irwin family. Senator Baker has been a member of the Museum's Board of Directors since the early days and his sage advice and wise counsel have been invaluable.

His stellar political career is legendary. He was the first popularly elected Republican senator in the state of Tennessee, and he rose quickly to serve as minority leader of the U. S. Senate, after which he became Senate majority leader. He was known among his colleagues as the "Great Conciliator" for his ability to broker compromises, enact legislation, and maintain civility. He served as a central figure in the notorious Watergate hearings, retiring from the Senate in 1985 in good standing. He was later called upon by President Ronald Reagan to serve as his chief of staff. He was then appointed by President George H. W. Bush as the U. S. ambassador to Japan, where he served for four years.

On July 14, 1998, the entire U. S. Senate honored Baker by assembling in the old Senate chamber, an

Former U.S. Senator Nancy Kassebaum Baker and Senator Howard H. Baker, Jr., relax on my back porch after a hearty dinner at our table where they enjoyed some of Elizabeth's home cooking. Nancy was the first woman elected to the U.S. Senate in her own right. (Photo taken by John Rice Irwin soon after the Bakers' marriage in 1996)

event that was attended by virtually every senator from both political parties, all of whom heaped praise on Baker. Howard Baker responded with a speech titled "Herding Cats," which referenced his days as Senate majority leader.

But Senator Baker's greatness does not lie exclusively in his illustrious career, but rather in the personal respect and genuine concern he exhibits for others. I had known about him and, of course, followed his career, and I was in awe of him, never thinking that we'd become acquainted and that he would become what I would describe as a close friend. But in the 1980s he brought his grandchildren to the Museum and after that he visited often and brought many of his friends. When our daughter Karen was killed in an automobile accident in 1999 he invited Elizabeth and me to come to his house. We spent the day touring the beautiful countryside, while experiencing the remarkable compassion of which he is capable.

But the main reason for including Senator Baker in this book of my history is to commemorate his priceless contributions to the Museum of Appalachia and to me personally. First and foremost, he agreed to become a member of the Board of Directors, not just in a titular role, but as an active and valued contributor to the work of the Museum. When there was dissension between me and the Board, several members resigned, but Howard (as well as Senator Alexander) stood by me all the way and was instrumental, in his legendary role as the "Great Conciliator," in bringing about harmony. There is not a single Board member, past or present, who does not have abiding respect and confidence in him. As I took a break from penning these lines, the following phrase kept creeping into my thoughts: "There's nothing in his heart but empathy, compassion, and civility."

His contributions to the Museum of Appalachia are legendary. Not only has he contributed financially, but he has helped with federal grants to the Museum. But his greatest contribution has been lending his name to the Board. He resigned membership from numerous other boards, some of national importance which paid him handsomely, but he remains a valuable and unpaid member of the Board of Directors of the Museum of Appalachia.

Alex Haley and His Years At The Museum

In January 1982, I received a telephone call from Governor Lamar Alexander asking me if I would meet with him and a small group of "historians," including Alex Haley, the writer. The group also included my friend Robin Hood, a noted photographer who, like Alex, was a Pulitzer Prize recipient. The purpose of the meeting was to discuss how the state could appropriately celebrate the upcoming bicentennial of Tennessee's admission to the Union. I readily agreed to attend. This invitation was the beginning of Alex Haley becoming the premier "salesman" for the Museum of Appalachia.

Alex Haley, the nation's celebrated writer of *Roots*, visited the Museum in 1982, where he built a house and stayed here periodically until his death in 1992. (Photo by Robin Hood, 1985)

I attended the informal meeting with the group in Nashville, and at lunch, we retired to a small restaurant, and by happenstance I was seated beside Alex Haley. Although we had never before met, we soon became "fast friends" and when Alex learned I had the Museum a few miles out of Knoxville I invited him to visit, and he said with an air of excitement, "You know, I'm scheduled to participate in the opening of the World's Fair there in Knoxville in a few weeks, and I'd love to visit your museum." Alex later admitted, mischievously, that in the back of his mind he was thinking, "Who wants to see another museum?"

On April 1, 1982, the day of the opening of the Fair, I located Alex in his hotel in Knoxville and re-invited him to visit the Museum. As I expected, he was totally booked for the day, and he seemed genuinely sorry that he had no spare time. "They have me booked for six interviews with newspapers, magazines, and television, including one with Tina Turner." Then he said, "Maybe I can combine some of these interviews, and if I can, I'll get back in touch with you." When I finished talking with him and hung up the telephone, I told Janice, my secretary, "Well, that is the last time I'll ever talk with Alex Haley." But to my surprise, Alex called me an hour later, stating that he had indeed combined several interviews and that he would have a few hours to visit the Museum if he had transportation, which I readily agreed to arrange.

As we strolled through the Museum grounds, Alex seemed genuinely mesmerized. Young lambs scampered hither and yon, trying to keep up with their mothers, and little chicks imitated the old hens in scratching the loose dirt for bugs beneath the cedar trees. The apple trees were in full bloom, as were the pear and peach trees. The lettuce, peas, and onions in the garden were lush, and Alex kept saying "Isn't this lovely; isn't this great!"

We went through several log cabins, each fully furnished in frontier, pioneer fashion, and finally we came to the old Peters Homestead and Thelma Phillips was there dressed in country garb, cooking pinto beans over the open fire, and baking cornbread in the cast iron baker. Alex seemed especially moved, reflecting, "I can just see my poor old grandma sitting there."

And as we meandered toward our house where Elizabeth had prepared a "hurried up" country meal, Alex said, once again, "Isn't this lovely!" He partook heavily of fried okra, mashed potatoes, turnip greens, cornbread and pinto beans, fried green tomatoes, and more. And when he finished, the few words that Alex uttered changed my life, and

his, and thousands of others. He politely asked if he could use our telephone and when he got Jackie, his secretary, on the line in Los Angeles, he said, "Jackie, I'm moving to Tennessee!" And from that point on he never wavered from this sudden, spur-of-the-moment resolve.

Alex asked me to look at various properties for him, notably a mansion/plantation in Middle Tennessee, and when we were viewing this ostentatious homestead, he started chuckling when we went into the main living room, the ceiling of which was covered with gold leaf. "What's so funny?" I asked him. He said he could sense the absurdity of him having a place of this grandeur, and that he could imagine what his poor old grandmother would say. "What WOULD she say?" I asked him. He retorted, without hesitation, "She would say, 'Son, have you done lost all your sense?', and I knew then that I would always feel uncomfortable in such regal surroundings."

It was at this point that Alex announced that he'd prefer a place near me and that maybe we could share the writing of some articles. He had read some of my books, most notably, *Alex Stewart, Portrait of a Pioneer*, and seemed impressed.

I had a secluded piece of land on Buffalo Creek adjacent to the Museum and he opted to buy this and build a house on it. When it was officially announced that Alex Haley was moving to East Tennessee, the press, both locally and nationally, covered it extensively. Keep in mind that Alex was doubtless the most popular writer in America, and that his book *Roots* had just been adapted and shown as a television series, which was generally described as the most watched program in broadcast history. My partner in real estate, Cathy Brown, and I soon sold Alex a large farm nearby, where two major creeks, the Buffalo and the Hinds, converged.

Alex commenced inviting national celebrities to his developed estate and to the Museum, and the resulting publicity, as far as the Museum was concerned, was incalculable. The editor-in-chief of *Reader's Digest*, the publisher of *Parade Magazine*, Brooke Shields, Oprah Winfrey, Quincy Jones, Lou Gossett, Jr., First Lady Hillary Clinton, Martha Stewart, and hundreds of others came.

Alex lived with Elizabeth and me in a tiny back room of our abode while his houses here were being finished (although he had homes in Los Angeles and in other places). He kept saying how friendly the people in East Tennessee were, and how much at home he felt, though he had never before lived in the Southern Appalachian Mountains (or even visited the area).

He and I traversed the rural areas of East Tennessee for several years. With Elizabeth and Knoxville TV news anchor Edye Ellis, among others, we traveled to New York and the headquarters of *Reader's Digest*, a trip which eventually resulted in the extensive article entitled "A Man and his Museum" in the June 1986 issue of the *Digest*. This was an eight-page piece, accompanied by several photos and written by the senior editor, Henry Hurt. When Henry, who had written extensively for *Reader's Digest* for forty years, was invited to speak at an international writers' conference in Tokyo, he chose this article as the subject of his speech.

Alex's contribution to the Museum was legendary. For example, he brought the entire board of the Parson's Foundation from Los Angeles and they decided (as they toured the Museum with Alex and me) that they would produce a one-hour documentary on the Museum of Appalachia and how and why it started. The film was produced over the next year and released nationwide to the Public Television Network. We attended the "premiere" at a plush hotel in Palm Springs, California.

He was responsible for bringing many foreign dignitaries to the Museum for extended visits, including Vitaly Korotich, the editor of *Ogonyok*, Russia's largest (and some say most important) newspaper. Korotich was given much credit for playing an important role in the historic breakup of the Soviet Union. A most charming, warm, and affable person, Vitaly spent a couple of days here, and I believe that he was one of the reasons we had our first "covered dish" supper.

At this supper, we had Fulton Ousler and more than a hundred other interesting celebrities. Walter Anderson, the editor of *Parade Magazine*, joined Korotich and Alex (at my request) to talk informally about how the U.S.S.R. and the U.S. could resolve their problems.

One of the most important contributions Alex made, in my opinion, occurred in the Cracker Barrel Restaurant in Caryville, Tennessee, in 1997. Along with Elizabeth and our daughter Elaine, we were having supper, and Alex was talking to Elaine about her future plans. "Why don't you come to the Museum and work for your Daddy?", he asked. Elaine agreed, and she has been a steadfast and diligent worker at the Museum ever since. Today, she is president of the Museum, and she is a tireless, dedicated, and most capable administrator and public relations person.

Brooke Shields created quite a stir when she visited here during the 1983 Tennessee Fall Homecoming. Writer Alex Haley looks on in the background.

Interesting and Colorful People Who Have Played a Part

The Cassidy Boys: The Kind and Friendly Brothers Who Met with Total Disaster

The Cassidy boys were of Irish descent, and were among seven children born to Dick and Betty Stooksbury Cassidy. Of the four boys, Tom, Harve, Jarve, and Lance moved back to the old Cassidy homeplace on the little dirt road in Beard Valley after World War II. The boys considered the old homeplace as their common headquarters, but they were free-spirited and independent, and each wanted his own place: quiet, isolated, and peaceful. Jarve had a tiny one-room frame house; Harve moved into an old trailer on the property; Lance stayed in the "big house;" and Tom got a tiny outbuilding from neighbors Odra and Artie Ailor and moved it to the old homeplace. It was edged into the woods, and faced a beautiful green meadow with the old homeplace visible in the distance. And there is where Tom spent the rest of his days, until his tragic death in 1989.

Oprah Winfrey was not only one of the nation's most popular celebrities, she was also one of the most gracious and friendly souls who visited the Museum. She is shown here in this photo with the writer.

Tom Cassidy sits on the "front porch" of his little house where he lived in peaceful solitude. I commented once on the size of his abode and he responded, "Well, I've got a cot, a little stove, a cooking pot and a frying pan, my fiddle (which his grandfather made), and a pistol—what more does a man need?" I moved his house to the Museum c. 1999, where it remains on display with a recording of Tom playing his grandfather's fiddle. (Photo by John Rice Irwin)

Brooke Shields is shown here with our Carlock Stooksbury and John Rice Irwin at the 1983 Homecoming event.

I remember Tom's response one time when I asked him about the little abode, which was the size of a "good-sized" bathroom: "I've got that little cot in there, a chair, a stove for heat and cooking, a frying pan, and bean pot, an old dresser, my fiddle (made by his grandfather Fate Cassidy), and my pistol. What more does a man need?" The several bullet holes in the roof were evidence that Tom had used the revolver to scare off marauding boys—or more likely, "the law."

Tom and his kin were great lovers of old-time mountain music, and Tom was considered to be a gifted singer. He played the guitar, mandolin, and fiddle, and he and his brother played for community gatherings from Knoxville, Tennessee, to Middlesboro and Lexington, Kentucky. His grandfather, Fate Cassidy, was a blacksmith, wagon maker, and legendary fiddle maker who crafted a fiddle for his neighbor, Roy Acuff, which was the first fiddle Roy ever had. Roy, universally heralded as the "King of Country Music," played this fiddle for some sixty years throughout most of the world.

The four brothers were gathered in the old homestead house one Saturday night, as they often did, to play music. It was a gay occasion, as usual, and the boys took turns playing and singing, and no doubt they were accompanied, as was their custom, by a jug of local moonshine. A disagreement arose over some trivial matter, and when the fracas ended, both Tom and one of his brothers lay dead. During a brief argument, Tom, in his inebriated state, pulled out his pocket knife and stabbed his brother Lance. When Tom realized he had killed his beloved brother, he grabbed a nearby loaded shotgun and killed himself.

It was a great shock to me and their neighbors and acquaintances; everyone liked the Cassidy boys, noted for their kind and friendly natures, their happy countenances, and the willingness, always, to lend a hand to a neighbor or even a stranger. When our daughter Karen was killed in a car wreck in 1999, we received several hundred letters of condolence. But the note which moved me the most was a crumpled letter, laboriously and crudely scrawled on a tablet leaf—from the two surviving Cassidy Boys.

My father, Glen Irwin, is shown here with my late daughter Karen, and my baby granddaughter Lindsey.

John Rice is shown here with his late daughter, Karen, on the day she graduated from the University of Tennessee.

Several years after this tragic event, I passed the old Cassidy place and noticed Tom's little house, abandoned and forlorn. I stopped at the main house and discovered that eighty-nine-year-old Harve was the only brother left on the grown-up old home place. I told him that I'd like to take the little house to the Museum in memory of old Tom and the Cassidy boys and he readily and anxiously agreed. The tiny abode sits here at the Museum today, furnished exactly as it was when Tom died; and as one stands on the front porch there plays a recording of Tom playing on the fiddle Fate Cassidy, his granddad, made for him.

Resting on the railing of her Foust Hollow cabin, Mary Bumgardner's face exudes kindness and contentment, as well as the deprivations and hardships she has endured on a tiny mountainside farm. The Museum's exhibits include several items from the Bumgardner family. (Photo by Gary Hamilton, 1982)

Alverta Stooksbury demonstrates clothes washing using homemade lye soap, a wooden wash board, and a "regular old galvanized tub." (Photo by Frank Hoffman)

Edna Scruggs, at left, and her sister-in-law, Sally Scruggs, are shown here at a Homecoming in the process of sulphuring apples in a large barrel (or hogshead) as a means of preserving them. (Photo by Frank Hoffman)

Granny Toothman learned to spin and weave in the little log cabin where she was born and reared in the mountains of Eastern Kentucky. She is shown here at work at one of the Museum's Homecomings. (Photo by Frank Hoffman)

W. G. "General" Lenoir

There was an older gentleman, W. G. "General" Lenoir, who lived less than a mile from my home and he was widely known as a collector of memorabilia of the region. He was reputed to have a "fabulous" collection of local and original artifacts. (He was not a military man; the nickname, General, came about because his great-grandfather was the locally noted Civil War General Lenoir of Lenoir City.)

One day, in my late teens, I paid a visit to the somewhat reclusive Lenoir and was enthralled at the fascinating and various agents of his collection. He was held in high esteem in the community. This inspired me to expand my efforts to emulate his endeavors.

Over the years General Lenoir and I developed a close friendship and although he was old enough in years to be my grandfather, he was young at heart. Our enthusiasm and our interest and excitement in acquiring relics of the past never waned—on the contrary, it only increased.

We often left in early morning and returned late at night, primarily traversing the back roads and country lanes of isolated mountain haunts, going from one homeplace to another. Our mutual interest and our enthusiasm for mountain relics were remarkable. At the end of each day, long after dark, we'd divide our day's acquisitions—he would take one item and I another until the day's take was depleted.

The "General" had visited many of the families in previous years and several others I had visited previously, but many were rank strangers to us. In such cases the art was to ingratiate ourselves to the family quickly.

It was most important to break the ice and "buy something" and pay in cash, whether or not we really valued the piece highly. We paid for it immediately, making sure that the potential seller knew we were "cash customers."

During the long drives with the General, we talked abstractly about philosophy, about the General's romantic life in the mountains, about his hog drives, and about his many experiences in years past. He became one of my closest friends and we enjoyed one another's company and experiences. He and I traveled the hinterland until a few weeks before he died in 1987 at the age of ninety-six.

When Lonnie Phillips left his mountain home, he carried a sack in which he gathered pieces of coal dropped from railroad cars. He would trade the coal to the villagers down in the valley for morsels of food, worn-out clothing, and various other items. (Photo by Gary Hamilton, 1980).

Lonnie pays attention as I count the greenbacks for the old shotgun he has made
from a water pipe and other discarded scraps. This photo was taken at the front door
of Lonnie's home. (Photo by Gary Hamilton, 1980)

Lonnie Phillips, Hermit of Briceville Mountain

"I reckon this mountain belongs to all of us."

I had heard stories of an old coal miner who had turned hermit and who lived alone and in total isolation at the top of a mountain near the coal mining town of Briceville in East Tennessee. There was no road nor lane leading to his abode and no one could give directions to his place—and only a handful of people had even been there anyway. Among those who thought they knew the way to his place were two of my friends: Squire Ray Beaty of Clinton and Floyd Wilson, a songwriter of some note.

We parked at an abandoned coal tipple at the foot of the mountain and found a faint foot path which led into the wilderness and almost straight up the precipitous ridge for what seemed like miles. At times the climb was so steep that we had to grab saplings to pull ourselves along the way. Finally we reached a serendipitous plateau area and three or four "stick" houses, which looked more like the work of seventh grade children than habitats for an adult.

When we neared the larger "brush" house, Lonnie, alerted by one of his emaciated dogs, came out, and before we could introduce ourselves Lonnie said, "Do you all want some gold?", and he reached into a pocket of one of his coats, producing a hand full of yellow metallic substance which he generously parceled out for each of us. Lonnie need not to have been embarrassed by his assumption, for "fool's gold" has long been mistaken for the real thing by gold prospectors (fool's gold is actually pyrite, a mineral containing iron and sulfur and closely resembling gold). But Lonnie didn't care whether or not it was real gold ore. It meant nothing to him, whether or not it was gold, or merely fool's gold.

Lonnie was a friendly "matter-of-fact" fellow who seemed happy enough, and content; one who talked to himself; and who answered our, and his, questions, but never initiated a conversation. He had buried anything he considered valuable, and like a squirrel he could find where each of his treasures were hidden, usually in old whiskey bottles, and covered with dirt and leaves. Once he stopped, suddenly, and scratched the leaves from an undisturbed area and brought out a shotgun of his own making, from a metal tube and other scrap parts. He was willing to sell it to me to get money for his snuff and tobacco. He had bottles buried randomly, each containing "important" papers of some sort. He loved tobacco and seemed to eat it religiously, rather than chew it as is customary.

On one of my subsequent visits, he was showing me where he had buried various items, and I asked him, "Lonnie, who does all this land belong to?", and he answered, in a true Socratic kind of way, "I reckon it belongs to all of us." (The "green" people would have been pleased). The mountain, I learned, belonged to one of the large absentee land companies that used it for the lumber and coal it produced.

A few paces from his main house, we noted evidence of a fire, obviously the remnants of one of Lonnie's earlier brush houses. The spot was surrounded by numerous spent shotgun shells and rifle cartridges, and I asked him what had happened. He answered with a single word, "snakes." I got a more explanatory answer later while talking with his son-in-law. He said the place was full of rattlesnakes and copperheads and that Lonnie slept there occasionally—a sort of summer home. Attempts by his son-in-law to rid the place of the poisonous reptiles were in vain, and over Lonnie's protests, his son-in-law set fire to the clutter which brought the snakes out in mass, and the casings and shells were evidence of some twenty-five snakes with which Lonnie had been living. He said they lived "in the walls," and had never bothered him.

The "house" that Lonnie built and lived in high on Briceville Mountain and miles from any neighbors. It contained only a dirt floor, no furnishings, no water, and he shared his home with copperheads and rattlesnakes, but he didn't fear them and was never bitten. (Photo by Gary Hamilton, 1980)

The first visit to Lonnie's place was in 1969, and I returned in 1978, and again in 1980 with my longtime friend and superb photographer, Gary Hamilton. In the interim, I learned more of Lonnie's background in a serendipitous manner. It goes as follows:

In 1962, as superintendent of schools in Anderson County, Tennessee, I visited a home in a remote section of the Cumberland Mountains to determine why none of the thirteen Phillips children were attending school. My attendance teacher, Margie Winstead, told me that many children were missing school because of a lack of clothing, and I wanted a firsthand look.

The house I visited consisted of only two ordinary-sized rooms, and both were nearly void of furniture. This, I later learned, was the home of Lonnie Phillips.

One room served as a kitchen, but it had only a tiny stove, a small table, a crude plank bench, and two or three chairs. The other room had two beds, a threadbare couch, and no heat. There was, of course, no inside plumbing, and I never knew the source of their water supply.

The house was dark, lighted only by one curtainless window. At first I didn't notice the contents of the big bed in the corner of the room, but as my eyes adjusted to the dim light, there slowly appeared the forms of six small bodies in the bed with only their heads peering from the quilts. The children were wide awake, perfectly still, and deathly quiet.

My assumption that the children were sick was quickly dispelled when their mother told me that they were in bed to keep warm. "We ain't got no heat, an' none of 'em have enough clothes to keep 'em warm, so hits jest keep 'em in bed 'er let 'em freeze. If it wasn't fer the bed kivers I guess we'd all freeze."

I never pass that little shotgun cabin hanging on the side of a steep bank without thinking of those children, lying there in the late afternoon, peering wide-eyed and silent from under the big patchwork quilt. And the quilt was the only colorful object in the otherwise drab and austere little house.

Twenty years later, in 1982, several of these same children visited me at the Museum and I was amazed at how healthy and prosperous they appeared to be. One was a postal employee in Birmingham; one was a school teacher in Ohio; and the others had respectable jobs and seemed to be well-adjusted middle-class citizens.

I had no idea that this large family of children was that of my old friend Lonnie Phillips, and one can imagine my surprise upon learning, many years later, of the connection. I don't know when and why Lonnie chose the life of a lonely hermit, presumably after some of his children were adults and on their own, but there was whispered talk that a neighbor man more forceful than the frail Lonnie had been pretty much in at the Phillips place on a permanent basis.

Years later, in February of 2010, I received a call from one Mary Phillips who identified herself as one of Lonnie's nine children, inquiring of me as to whether or not I had a photo of her father, who had died a few years earlier. I was somewhat shocked when she told me that she had lived on the mountain with Lonnie for a short while. Mary was well-spoken and articulate and I was anxious to meet her. I invited her to come by the Museum here in Norris for lunch. The following are some notes taken during her brief visit here.

I had thought of Lonnie often over the years, and I can see the silhouette of his mountain from my home, some twenty miles to the west. One night the temperature dropped to an unprecedented twenty-four degrees below zero Fahrenheit, and I wondered how Lonnie had managed to keep warm in his dirt-floored abode, with little protection from the cold winds. I thought, too, that from Lonnie's perch he could see the distant lights of Oak Ridge, referred to as the birthplace of atomic energy—and a town which boasted of having the highest ratio of scholars and PhDs of any city in the country. And I thought maybe Lonnie was just as happy and content and satisfied with his freedom as the eminent international scientists and engineers who lived so near. Lonnie, like so many who lived in the Southern Appalachian Mountains, cherished his freedom and abhorred laws and regulations. He seemed happy and content and at peace with nature, the world around him, and with himself.

Gene Purcell

This gentle soul knows and loves the mountains, the streams, and the meadows of Southern Appalachia more than anyone I know. Gene lives alone in his Wolf Valley home a few miles south of the Museum with his fabulous collection of Indian and early pioneer relics. He is easily the most accommodating and giving soul I've ever known, and he is perhaps my closest friend, and one who is responsible for literally thousands of items now displayed in the Museum. Many of the pieces were donated, outright, by him and hundreds of others I purchased from Gene for nominal prices. He was influenced mightily by his grandfather, with whom he spent most of his growing-up years. They fished, trapped, and hunted together, worked in the woods, tended gardens and the farm, but mainly they were together in all their endeavors. Today, no matter the subject of conversation, Gene will always get around to referring to his grandfather, one way or another. His admiration for his grandfather verges on worship for the venerable old man.

Gene has spent much of his life scouring the environs of East Tennessee and adjacent states, collecting an impressive array of Indian, early military, country, and pioneer relics. He is a substantive student of Southern Appalachia and has been my companion in traversing the mountains for literally thousands of miles. I cannot think of a single individual more knowledgeable, more giving, and less selfish than my longtime and loving confidant. Hundreds of the items in the Museum today are a direct result of his generous assistance.

In addition to the plethora of physical artifacts for which Gene is responsible for the Museum acquiring, he has donated some twenty-five years of part-time volunteer guidance and labor. He is the person we always go to for advice and consultation, and for the ultimate word on almost any subject.

Gene Purcell, John Rice's closest friend and the Museum's unpaid benefactor and advisor extraordinaire, is shown here on the veranda of the Hall of Fame at the Museum.

Alex Stewart

Alex Stewart may well be the most interesting, fascinating, knowledgeable, and endearing man I have ever known. He certainly contributed more to the various aspects of the ideals that ARE the Museum of Appalachia than anyone else.

I shall not attempt to describe in detail, or to characterize him here, since I have written an extensive book on his life, *Alex Stewart, Portrait of a Pioneer* is available at the Museum gift shop, at bookstores around the country, and online at Amazon.com. The book has been in print and available nationwide since it was first published in 1985. It is also distributed in several countries.

I can truthfully say that my story of this little mountain man has brought me more accolades and compliments than any of my other endeavors, with the possible exception of the Museum itself. And at the risk of appearing overly immodest, I can state that a vast majority of the people who have read the book have told me that they considered it the best book they had ever read, and many stated that they had read it through more than once. Valty Maloney of Hancock County, Tennessee, vowed that he had read it through nine times.

My friend, Senator Lamar Alexander, called me from his Washington, D. C., office in December 2000, and in the course of our conversation informed me that he had purchased and sent to his friends 400 copies of the Alex Stewart book.

Alex Stewart was perhaps the most remarkable person I've ever met. I was so impressed with him that I wrote a book on his life: *Alex Stewart, Portrait of a Pioneer*; I consider it to be one of my most notable accomplishments. He is shown here finishing a cedar butter churn at his Hancock County, Tennessee, home. We have an extensive exhibit on Alex and his wares in the Hall of Fame here at the Museum. (Photo by Frank Hoffman, c. 1977)

Levi Collins of Bear Creek Hollow was a farmer, miller, blacksmith, moonshiner, and all-around mountain man who worked occasionally at the Museum. He is shown here with the Museum's twin oxen, Jacob and Esau. Esau is hidden behind his brother.

Ray King, at right, and Paul Ault, from whom I bought many unusual antiques, are typical mountain traders from the Cumberland Plateau region of Central Tennessee. Careful observation will reveal that Paul's left hand holds a billfold so filled with large bills that it won't close. (Photo by my friend and Pulitzer Prize recipient, Robin Hood, c. mid-1970s)

Carlock Stooksbury was able to compete with the great bluegrass bands with his simple $4.00 mouth bow made for us by the great Alex Stewart. Carlock is shown here playing at one of our Homecoming events. (Photo by Frank Hoffman)

Minnie Black, who grew, made, and played musical instruments made of gourds, is shown here with the renowned fiddler Charlie Acuff at one of the Museum's Homecoming festivals.

Three of the better known and most respected former U. S. senators had an informal cup of coffee in my office here at the Museum to discuss old times when they were serving in the Senate. From left are: former Tennessee Senator Howard H. Baker, Jr.; his wife, former Kansas Senator Nancy Kassebaum Baker, the first woman elected to the U. S. Senate not following a father or husband; and former Wyoming Senator Allen Simpson, who is highly renowned as an outspoken sage of past Senators, and who now (in 2011) is frequently in the national news as vice-chair of the "famous gang of six" designated to fix the budget crisis.

When Governor Lamar Alexander started to plan for the celebration of Tennessee's 200th birthday in 1978, he chose this august group to plan and participate in it. Some of the most outstanding Tennesseans in the state, they assembled here at the Museum for their first meeting. They are, from left to right: the noted writer, Wilma Dykeman; Governor Alexander; Minnie Pearl, whom Alexander described as the second most recognized comedian in the country; Alex Haley, the most famous writer in America at the time; Governor Ned Ray McWherter, two-time Governor of Tennessee, and later a powerful figure in National politics; and Lieutenant Governor John Wilder, who, for some fifty years, was a powerhouse in Tennessee politics. (Photo by Robin Hood, 1980)

Alex Haley visited the Museum at the height of his phenomenal career and fell in love with the Museum and with the people of Tennessee. He decided to build a home near the Museum. He is shown here at left, far back in the mountains, buying wooden figures from the Partin-Webb family. Judy Partin-Webb is shown in the center. (Photo by Frank Hoffman, mid 1980's)

Chapter XII

Some Accolades Along the Way

I'll not bore the reader by listing the dozens of various awards and honors we have received over the years, but I will modestly list a few.

Museum of Appalachia Becomes Smithsonian Affiliate

Certainly one of the most important and prestigious honors received by the Museum of Appalachia was the invitation to become an official affiliate of the Smithsonian Institution in Washington, D. C. Harold Closter, director of Smithsonian Affiliations, made the announcement on May 20, 2007, at a ceremony held at the Museum. In a letter to me on October 18, 2006, prior to the event, Closter stated, "You have created a true American treasure. The whole operation clearly reflects your passion and commitment to preserving the heritage and spirit of the people of Appalachia."

The event was attended by the Museum Board of Directors, the Advisory Board, and several guests. Closter was introduced by Museum Board of Directors member Senator Howard H. Baker, Jr.

Closter, who initially toured the Museum at the suggestion of Senator Baker, almost immediately invited the Museum to become a member of the Smithsonian Affiliate program. In making the presentation, Closter said, "The Smithsonian is delighted to welcome the Museum of Appalachia into our affiliate program. The Museum of Appalachia has done a remarkable job of preserving the legacy of America's early history. Our affiliate relationship will help advance the understanding of this important heritage."

He stated further, "The Museum of Appalachia ... has done a remarkable job of educating the public about the life, history, and culture and contributions of the people of East Tennessee. This is a story that provides inspiration to all Americans and to many around the world."

On May 23, 2007, Dr. Harold Closter, at left, director of Smithsonian Affiliations, Smithsonian Institution, presents John Rice Irwin with formal recognition of the Museum as an official Smithsonian Affiliate. (Photo by Dick Doub, 2007)

I stated at the ceremony that the affiliation was another milestone in the Museum's growth and improvement. The affiliation includes partnerships with the Smithsonian's outreach units, including community outreach workshops, lectures, curriculum development in local schools, study tours, and an internship program. The Smithsonian also hosts a national conference for affiliates every summer.

The Associated Press released a story of our affiliation and this provided favorable publicity for the Museum across the country. I could not help but be humbled when I recalled the little pile of antiques, covered with a borrowed tarpaulin, from which the Museum had grown in just a few short years!

The MacArthur (Genius) Award

Easily the most prestigious and important award I received was the MacArthur Award, commonly referred to as the "Genius" Award. This is an award for which the recipient cannot apply, nor even be aware that he or she is being considered. The short version is that I received a telephone call one day informing me that I had been nominated to receive this award, which had been presented to only a handful of people from the entire nation. The extended amount of the award was some $260,000, in cash, with no strings attached. The only question was whether or not I would accept. I need not inform the Foundation how or where I expended the money, nor respond to them in any way. The only question for me was whether or not I would accept the award. Needless to say, I did answer in the affirmative.

I am not one to be demonstrative or to show emotions, and when I ended the conversation, my longtime secretary and assistant, Andrea Fritts, asked me, "Who was that?" And I responded without excitement, or exhilaration, "That was the MacArthur Foundation and they are giving me the 'Genius' award, along with $260,000." I did not know who nominated me, or who shepherded my name through the long selection process, although I suspected two or three celebrities who may have been responsible. One was the great writer, Cormac McCarthy. (Cormac has been described by various critics as the best writer on the American scene today. He is the recipient of the Pulitzer Prize for literature and numerous other awards.)

This award made the news in places such as New York City, Los Angeles, and in other large metropolitan newspapers, but not so much locally. The proceeds from this prestigious and financial windfall I put into developing the Museum; none went to my personal coffers.

Other Awards and Honors

I was the recipient of an Honorary Doctorate from Cumberland College and later a Doctor of Letters from Lincoln Memorial University. When I returned home from receiving these Doctorates, the outside workers at the Museum said, "When we get hurt or sick we won't have to go to our doctors anymore. John Rice has two doctors' degrees and he can doctor us—no need to go to any other doctors!"

I've received several statewide awards and two or three national awards, but the one that I'm most proud of is the local Norris Lion's Club's designation of me as "Man of the Year" because it was presented by my neighbors. I've had the honor of speaking before dozens (maybe hundreds) of groups at colleges, universities, civic groups, and two special groups in Washington and even at West Point Military Academy. My band accompanied me on many of these engagements and interspersed the speaking with musical interludes.

Chapter XIII

The Day I Gave the Museum Away

Most of my life has been devoted to developing the Museum, and it became successful far beyond any expectations that I could have fathomed. Why, then, would I give it away—the land, the buildings, the many thousands of artifacts? That is the question universally asked.

The answer to that question is rather simple. The Museum had grown to such proportions that I could no longer afford the ever-increasing maintenance and upkeep costs. My primary goal was for the Museum to remain open for the public and I thought that a reputable non-profit corporation could do this. First, this non-profit corporation could receive certain grants from federal, state, and local governments, and from corporate foundations and individuals, but I could not qualify for such monies as a sole proprietorship. It was the most dramatic and gut-wrenching decision I ever made.

My first concern was that my daughter Elaine (and her three children, Lindsey, John, and Will) would benefit from these assets, valued at millions of dollars. But the Museum was losing money every day as most museums do, and I was keeping it afloat by putting my personal resources into it.

My youngest grandson, Will Meyer, has been around the Museum since he was a small tyke. (Photo by John Rice Irwin, January, 1998)

Elaine Irwin Meyer, Museum president and executive director, and her father, John Rice Irwin, founder of the Museum. (Photo by Ninette Campbell).

The cutting of the ribbon on the day John Rice Irwin gave the Museum to a non-profit corporation. Left to right, Bill Henry, Sam Furrow, John Rice Irwin, Tennessee Governor Lamar Alexander, Elaine Meyer, and granddaughter Lindsey Meyer.

I reached a point where I could no longer "feed" the Museum and I didn't want to see its demise, and I reasoned that a non-profit, tax-exempt corporation would be the most likely means of keeping it afloat. The Museum remains open and viable today, but the 2011 Board is struggling mightily in order to keep it open. The day that I actually transferred the Museum from my private ownership to a non-profit Board stands as one of the most somber moments of my life.

The day was clear and hot, and a large crowd had gathered at the Museum for the "celebration" of my giving it away. But to me the occasion was more like a funeral gathering than a celebration. My wife, Elizabeth, was there, as was our daughter, Elaine, and her husband, Ed Meyer, and my three grandchildren. I was giving away much of their legacy, but they all stood there with expressions of something between stoicism and sadness. There was a large ribbon that was about to be cut simultaneously by myself, Governor Lamar Alexander, a host of friends, and the family, thus formally consummating the transfer.

Lamar Alexander, who was the incoming chairman of the Board of Directors, had given me one last chance to change my mind, but I felt that I had no alternative but to carry forth, and that is what happened. It was soon over and that was that. My lifelong creation, the result of decades of blood, sweat, and tears, was no longer mine.

The Board of Directors

The Museum has been exceedingly fortunate to have attracted outstanding members to serve on its Board of Directors. They are, past and present:

Senator Lamar Alexander, first chairman of the Museum of Appalachia Board of Directors; current U.S. senator, and former Tennessee governor, president of the University of Tennessee, and U. S. secretary of education

Judge Riley Anderson, former chief justice of the Tennessee Supreme Court

Hack Ayers, prominent businessman and land developer in East Tennessee

Senator Howard H. Baker, Jr., one of America's leading statesmen and former U.S. senator, Senate majority leader, ambassador to Japan, chief of staff for President Ronald Reagan

Sandy Beall, founder and owner of Ruby Tuesday national chain of restaurants

Glen Bolling, political and community leader

Dail Cantrell, local attorney

Pete Claussen, prominent railroad magnate and former chairman of the Museum Board of Directors

Jim Clayton, founder of Clayton Homes and listed by Forbes Magazine as one of the 200 most wealthy men in America

David Coffey, businessman, philanthropist, and former Tennessee state representative

Jay Crippin, prominent businessman and industrialist

Mike Evans, business leader and national distributor of Beretta weapons

Daryl Fansler, prominent Knoxville attorney and chancellor of the Knox County, Tennessee, Chancery Court

Sam Furrow, leading Knoxville businessman and realtor and former chairman of the Museum Board of Directors

Natalie Haslam, prominent Knoxville philanthropist and wife of Jim Haslam, founder of Pilot Oil Company

Tom Hill, local newspaper publisher

Dan Holbrook, prominent Knoxville attorney and estate planner

Marsha Hollingsworth, businesswoman and philanthropist

John Rice Irwin, author, educator, businessman, and founder and developer of the Museum of Appalachia

Dr. Joe Johnson, former president of the University of Tennessee and former chairman of the Museum Board of Directors

Joe La Grone, farm boy from East Texas who became manager of Oak Ridge operations for the Department of Energy, with 26,000 employees in Oak Ridge, Tennessee, and in Kentucky and Ohio

Elaine Irwin Meyer, daughter of John Rice Irwin and current president of the Museum of Appalachia

Harry Moskos, former editor, Knoxville News-Sentinel

Rex Henry Ogle, circuit court judge in Sevier County, Tennessee

Manya Pirkle, noted artist, philanthropist, and businesswoman

Gene Purcell, noted authority on antiques and local history

James B. "Buddy" Scott, Jr., retired circuit court judge for Anderson County and former chairman of the Museum Board of Directors

General Carl Stiner, retired United States Army four-star general, now serving as a military consultant

Billy Stokes, Knoxville attorney

Gary Wade, chief justice of the Tennessee Supreme Court

The Museum has also been blessed with a strong and active Board of Advisors:

Dr. William Acuff, retired chief of staff, UT Hospital, Baptist Health System

Glenn Bowling, Claiborne County commissioner

Tom Carpenter, international philanthropist and contributor to the Museum

Pete Claussen, Knoxville railroad magnate who joined the Advisory Board after his tenure as a Museum director

Steve Dean, television producer and creator of the acclaimed "The Heartland Series"

Edye Ellis, popular television broadcaster and consultant

Fred Fields, retired attorney

Larry Foster, director of Anderson County schools

Dr. Charles Gouffon, *retired orthopedic surgeon*

Hallerin Hilton Hill, *Knoxville radio personality*

Richard Ladd, *attorney and former judge in Bristol, Tennessee*

Fred Marcum, *aide to Senator Howard H. Baker, Jr.*

Bo Schaffer, *insurance executive*

William Stokely, *principal in the national Stokely/Van Camp Corporation*

Pat Summitt, *women's head basketball coach at the University of Tennessee*

Jack Williams, *retired vice president for development, University of Tennessee*

By unanimous consent of the Board, my daughter, Elaine Irwin Meyer, has served as executive director, then president, of the Museum. She has fulfilled these roles in a dedicated and exemplary manner.

My daughter Elaine, executive director of the Museum, at left, and her mother and my wife, the late Elizabeth Irwin.

Chapter XIV
The Museum Today

It may be appropriate, in describing the Museum, to borrow a line from Charles Dickens' *A Tale of Two Cities*: "It was the best of times, and the worst of times ...."

In regard to the good times, one could point to the beautiful and well-manicured grounds and gardens, to the pastoral flocks of sheep, the herd of fainting goats, and the flocks of ducks, chickens, peafowl, and guineas that roam the environs at will. We could point to four large, multi-story display buildings, and to a total of forty-seven authentic log cabins and houses, two grist mills, a school, a church, and various other smaller structures, all reconstructed with an eye for authenticity. We should emphasize, as well, the artifacts displayed in these structures in an effort to project the quality of life in the heyday of the buildings, which portrays the stories and the histories of the people who made, mended, cared for, and used them, and then passed them on to their sons and daughters. After all, the untold thousands of relics, each with a story, and each relating to a family or an individual, is what the Museum was, and is, all about.

Kate and Bonnie, the Museum mules, graze peacefully among the green grass and spring buttercups near the Museum entrance drive. The Old Graham House is in the background. (Photo by Dick Doub).

The overhang, or cantilever, barn shown in the background is unique to the East Tennessee area. The sheep are a part of the flock that roams the Museum grounds. (Photo by Jim Marziotti)

These fainting goats are among the many animals that roam the Museum grounds. The Old Graham House, in the background, is one of some sixty structures in the Museum. (Photo by Nell Moore).

One of the early spring gardens at the Museum is shown here, with the Display Barn and the People's Building in the background. Both these buildings contain extensive displays of the Southern Appalachian region and its people. (Photo by Dick Doub)

This old hen forages the Museum grounds with her newly-hatched chicks.

Such familiar publications as the *Reader's Digest, Smithsonian Magazine, National Geographic, The Atlanta Constitution, The Los Angeles Times, Southern Living Magazine*, and virtually every major newspaper in the United States has published feature articles about the Museum. In addition, the three main television networks have come to the Museum and have carried news briefs, and a bevy of cable channels, including the History Channel and PBS, have carried documentaries and continue to do so. Three movie crews have filmed major made-for-TV movies on the premises, including "Young Dan'l Boone," "Christy," and "The Work and the Glory: Pillar of Light." PBS filmed its three-part series, "The Appalachians," on site at the Museum, and the Parsons Foundation of Los Angeles produced a one-hour documentary about me and the Museum that was one year in the making. It premiered while we were present in Palm Springs, California, and was released nationally for broadcast on PBS stations.

The number of conferences, seminars, social meetings, reunions, and weddings conducted at the Museum are increasing, both in the auditorium, on the outside stage, and in various other buildings and open-air locations. As mentioned earlier, the Museum is an official affiliate of the Smithsonian Institute in Washington, D.C., and the importance of this connection can hardly be over-emphasized.

Another aspect of the "best of times" is the good will and public acceptance that the Museum enjoys. We have a large gift and craft shop featuring thousands of handmade items by local and regional artisans, and our accompanying restaurant serves regional food that is popular with locals and visitors alike. Ninety-nine percent of those who visit the Museum heap praise and even adoration on the facility; and the same is true regarding the press.

The Museum jackass is shown here relaxing in the sheep pen on a lazy afternoon. (Photo by John Rice Irwin).

This mother and daughter are from a very small breed, known as "fainting" or "nervous" goats. Any sudden or loud noise often causes the entire herd to fall prostrate on the ground for a few minutes. The cause of this phenomenon remains a mystery.

The goat on top of the large hay bale figured out a way to feed undisturbed by her kin. (Photo by Gary Hamilton)

But the impact of the museum upon the multitudes of visitors that we see daily continues to be the most important and most constant measure of our success. This brings to mind an event that took place just this past summer, It was almost dark on Saturday, July 2, 2011, when Don and Sara Jane Dunn of Alabama pulled into the Museum of Appalachia parking lot. The Museum had closed for the day, and a lone caretaker was trying to finish mowing before the last vestiges of light faded away.

The Dunns were not surprised to find the Museum closed. They had spent the entire day here, and had returned after supper "just to see what the Museum looked like in the evening twilight."

The lone caretaker was my grandson, John Rice Irwin Meyer, and he was more interested in finishing his work than in visiting with "just some more tourists." However, he dutifully and patiently spoke with the couple for some thirty minutes because of their manifest fascination with the Museum. They queried Little John (as my grandson is called in the family) about the Museum and especially about the founder of this "remarkable place." Reluctantly but proudly, Little John told them his grandfather had personally founded and developed the Museum.

Don Dunn asked my grandson if there was any possibility of meeting the founder. Little John, who has always been protective of me, said I'd recently undergone surgery and had just returned from the hospital—but I might feel like talking the following day. Although the Dunns had planned to leave early the next morning for their home near Birmingham, they asked my grandson to see if I felt up to visitors.

Don and Sara Jane agreed to meet Little John the next morning at 9 a.m. when the Museum opened. When John arrived, the Dunns were waiting for him.

John was so impressed with the couple that he took the morning off to "re-tour" with them; then they came to my house after lunch.

The Dunns were easily the friendliest, most appreciative, and most complimentary folks I had met in a long time. Don said that if he had visited the Museum when he was "fresh out of high school," his life-long mission would have been to create a similar museum in his area.

The Dunns left my house in mid-afternoon—and soon afterward Don wrote Little John a letter saying that "these were the two most pleasant days of my life." The Dunns and my grandson have corresponded several times, and Little John has talked incessantly of Don and Sara.

I must say that the most important result of this entire incident is the effect it had on my grandson. He saw the Museum complex through the eyes of people who appreciated it to the utmost. And the fact that they were so greatly impressed, so in awe of what they had seen, gave John a new appreciation of the Museum—a place with which he's been familiar his entire life—and this gave me the greatest pleasure.

Behind these "best of times" lurks the "worst of times" that must be considered. One word tends to summarize the latter: finances. As the Museum has expanded and grown, so too have the maintenance and operating costs. The original buildings, some more than two centuries old, need continual upkeep and the grounds and gardens, complete with a generous animal population, are expensive to maintain. Even with vigilant, constant, and careful management, the expenditures tend to outweigh the income from entrance fees and contributions. But notwithstanding, we are optimistic that the Museum of Appalachia can and will survive for the purposes for which it was intended.

Sheep graze peacefully underneath a blossoming apple tree at the "Little Overhang" barn at the Museum. (Photo by John Rice Irwin)

The little Chapel in the Wildwood where old time harp singing is still performed, on occasions, as well as wedding services and hymn singing. I modestly named it Irwin's Chapel because the original name of the chapel was not known in the North Carolina mountains from where I acquired it.

Winter scene of Irwin Chapel Church.

Nancy and Russ Rose worked at the Museum off and on for several years. Several of their
fine baskets are on permanent display in the Museum's Hall of Fame.

Mule-powered sorghum grinding during the annual Museum of Appalachia Tennessee Fall Homecoming is a popular demonstration.

The Loom House
In some old homesteads where there were several spinsters (unmarried girls), a separate small building was constructed for their spinning wheels, looms, and other textile-related accoutrements; it was called a "loom house." This one is located near the Peters Homestead House in the Museum. (Photo by Robin Hood).

We read almost daily of the distress of other museums, both large and small; some are reducing hours and several are closing permanently. I know of four respected and viable museums within less than 100 miles of our Museum that have totally closed. But, to reiterate, we're optimistic that, with the support of our friends and visitors, we will not only survive, but will grow and expand.

In the past few years, we've added two new buildings: the Tom Cassidy House and Gwen Sharp's Little Playhouse. The Hacker Martin Grist Mill adjacent to the Museum is unfinished; perhaps in the long term it may be placed in working order. A fitting project for a museum of Appalachian history would be a replica of a coal mine and associated exhibits. Alex Stewart's cabin could be renovated and opened for visitors. These and other projects will keep the Museum alive, exciting, and vibrant for new and returning visitors.

Above all, I have sought to tell the stories of the Appalachian people, in their own words and through the artifacts they've left behind. The Museum of Appalachia is my tribute to the warm, friendly, and hardworking people of our region. It is my life's work and my legacy—and it is my hope that the Museum will continue to thrive and grow through the rest of my lifetime and beyond.

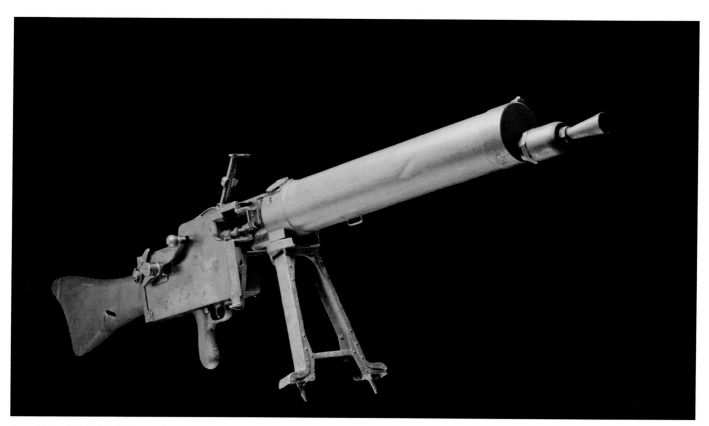

Sgt. Alvin C. York Machine Gun
This .30 Caliber machine gun is authenticated to be one of the most historic items of World War I. It was acquired on October 8, 1918, by Sgt. Alvin C. York of nearby Pall Mall, Tennessee, when he led an attack on a German machine gun nest, killing 28 German soldiers and capturing 132 others. Sgt. York has been widely described as the most outstanding hero of the war. The author, John Rice Irwin, spent more than a year acquiring and authenticating this weapon.

The Irwins, the late Elizabeth and John Rice, on an autumn stroll through the Museum.
(Photo by Dick Doub).

My cousin, eighty-five-year-old Bonnie Carden, teaches my granddaughter, Lindsey Meyer, to quilt. (Photo by Pulitzer Prize Photographer Robin Hood).

Nancy and Russ Rose made baskets here at the Museum for years, and one day I told them I wanted them to make the world's biggest white oak splint basket. This is the result of a summer's work. It is on permanent display here at the Museum in the Hall of Fame. Our grandchildren, John and Lindsey Meyer, find plenty of room in the basket, and in the background is my wife Elizabeth, noted singer and fiddler Ramona Jones, our daughter Elaine, and the nationally celebrated Grandpa Jones, longtime star of the Grand Ole Opry and the popular TV series, "Hee Haw."

Index